THE TEX-MEX GRILL

and

Backyard Barbacoa
Cookbook

MEXICAN COWBOYS washing up after round-up on a cattle ranch near Marfa, 1939

the Tex-GRILL

Mex

and
BACKYARD
Barbacoa COOKBOOK

Robb Walsh

BROADWAY BOOKS
NEW YORK

TAILGATERS GRILLING fajitas before a University of Texas Longhorns football game in Austin

mation

Sprinkler &
c Gate Systems

nd Service
89

BROADWAY

Published in the United States by Broadway Books,
an imprint of the Crown Publishing Group,
a division of Random House, Inc., New York.
www.crownpublishing.com

BROADWAY BOOKS and the Broadway Books colophon
are trademarks of Random House, Inc.

Portions of this book first appeared in different forms in the *Houston Press* (or
houstonpress.com), a Village Voice Media publication.

Library of Congress Cataloging-in-Publication Data
Walsh, Robb
  The Tex-Mex grill & backyard barbacoa cookbook/by Robb Walsh. — 1st ed.
    p. cm.
1. Barbecue cookery—Texas. 2. Barbecue cookery—Mexico, North. I. Title.
  TX840.B3W3625 2010
  641.5'78409764—dc22   2010002881

ISBN 978-0-7679-3073-4

PRINTED IN THE UNITED STATES OF AMERICA

Design by Erin Mayes, EmDash

10 9 8 7 6 5 4 3 2 1

FIRST EDITION

For Katie and Julia,
with love and hot sauce

FIDEL CASTRO samples Texas beef at a barbecue restaurant while on a goodwill trip to Houston in 1959

Contents

Acknowledgments

THANKS TO THE TEX-MEX LEGENDS WHO gave me their time, including Victor Leál, Joe Alonso, Jorge Cortez, Sonny Falcon, Christy Carrasco, David Garrido, Melissa Guerra, Robert Amaya, the late Mama Ninfa, and the late Matt Martinez Jr. Many thanks to chef Guillermo González Beristáin in Monterrey for his help and hospitality. Thanks to Dr. Jeff Savell and Dr. Davey Griffin of the Meat Science Section of the Department of Animal Science, Texas A&M University, for teaching me where fajitas come from. Thanks to my wife, Kelly Klaasmeyer, for editing, recipe critiques, sage advice, and babysitting. Thanks to my agent, David McCormick, for making it happen. Thanks to Erin Mayes for design work and for going above and beyond. Thanks to Christina Malach at Random House for taking the reins. Thanks to Catherine Matusow and Katharine Shilcutt for moral support.

Thanks to Margaret Downing and my employers for permission to use the photos, text, recipes, and articles first published by the *Houston Press* (or houstonpress.com), a Village Voice Media publication.

Introduction

FROM THE MESQUITE FIRES OF THE SPAN-
ish vaqueros to the taco trucks of modern *taqueros,*
no American regional cuisine has contributed more
to the nation's grilling style than Tex-Mex. And no
one is more fanatical about grilling and barbecue-
ing than the people who inhabit the bicultural bor-
derlands of Texas and northern Mexico.

Grilling has long been a part of the lifestyle of the
cattle raisers who settled this region. And while it
was mostly replaced by frying and stewing in early
Tex-Mex, grilling has experienced a revival. Since the
1970s, fajitas and other grilled meats and seafoods
have slowly replaced combo platters as the most popular food in Tex-Mex restaurants and cantinas.

At the same time, the American love affair with the
grill has been rekindled. In the twenty-first century,
the backyard barbecue has become emblematic of
American cookery. It is our connection to the mem-
ory of what makes our food American. The word
"barbecue" comes from the Spanish *barbacoa*; both
are words derived from the name that native Americans gave their grills. The *barabicu* of the indigenous
Americans was a grate of green sticks used to sus-
pend meat or fish over smoldering coals.

In the 1600s, European explorers on the island
of Hispaniola marveled at this unfamiliar cooking
method and were baffled by its inefficiency. They
couldn't figure out why the Native American hunters and fishermen were content to lie in their ham-
mocks for hours watching the meat and fish cook
slowly over smoldering coals. From the perspective
of those of us who cook outdoors for recreation, the
simultaneous use of the hammock and the barbecue makes perfect sense.

Whether it burns propane, charcoal, or wood,
the modern backyard grill is directly descended
from the barabicu of the first Americans. And every
twenty-first-century tailgater, cook-off competitor,
and backyard barbecuer who grills for the sheer joy
of it is an heir to that tradition.

Over the last half century, Tex-Mex grilling has
evolved into an eye-popping spectacle of grilled
meats and seafoods served on sizzling *comals*. And
the bold-flavor signature of dried chili powder rubs
and fresh chile pepper salsas has inspired legions
of backyard barbecuers to adopt the borderland
grilling style.

I hope this book encourages you to get out your
grill. I also hope it puts you in closer touch with the
foodways of Texas and northern Mexico and brings
some exciting new flavors to your table. Most of all,
I hope it makes your next fiesta a lot of fun.

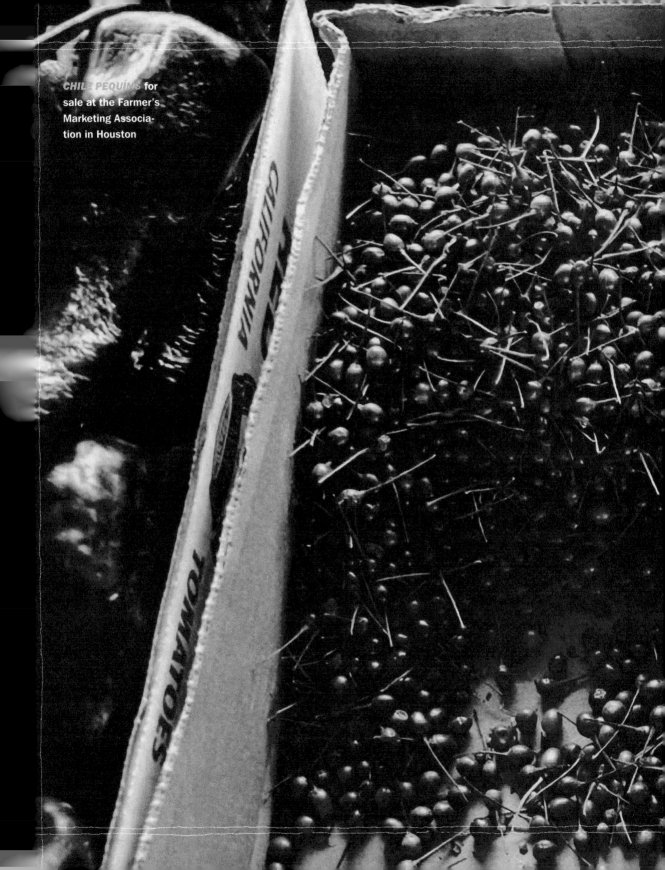

CHILE PEQUINS for sale at the Farmer's Marketing Association in Houston

#1

MESQUITE WOOD AND CHILE PEQUÍNS

GO DOWN CALLE 8 AND LOOK FOR THE *CABRITOS* cooking on spits in the window. That's the easy way to find Los Norteños, my favorite restaurant in Matamoros, a Mexican border town across the Rio Grande from Brownsville. The last time I was there, I sat at a table near the grill and made cabrito (baby goat) tacos. I started with a layer of loin meat and some thin kidney slices that I showered with salt. Then I added raw onion and a little lettuce and squeezed a lime wedge over it. I topped this with some *pico de gallo*, being careful not to load the pliant fresh corn tortilla beyond its rolling point. They were magnificent tacos.

It was May 1, Mexico's Labor Day. There was a big parade in downtown Matamoros, and a lot of people were out celebrating. I had been visiting the busy street vendors' stalls all day, eating tacos and taking notes about grilling. Now I was glad to sit down and relax at a real dining table in an air-conditioned restaurant.

Cabrito al pastor, cabrito turned on a metal spit over mesquite coals, is a technique so revered in northern Mexico that it has been adapted to fit elegant restaurants. At Los Norteños and many upscale restaurants in Monterrey, the brick fire pit that holds the pungent mesquite coals and the aromatic goats is separated from the dining room by a wall of thick glass.

Founded in 1950, Los Norteños is a restaurant relic. The dozen or so dark wood tables in the downstairs dining room are patrolled by four mustachioed waiters in jackets and ties. The manager is a white-haired guy named Ignacio who everybody calls "Nacho." He stands up front near the door at an old-fashioned wooden cashier stand that looks like a pulpit decorated with big glass jars full of candy.

I ordered the *riñonada* portion of the cabrito, which included ribs, some tender loin meat, and the kidney. First I was served a bowl of bean soup and some tortilla chips. Then the waiter brought over a huge stack of hot tortillas in a wicker basket, and a plate with lettuce, tomato, and raw onions. A bowl of hellishly hot pico de gallo with big hunks of raw serrano in it arrived, along with another bowl of a milder cooked salsa. When I finished the soup, my plate of cabrito arrived. The whole spread cost around twelve dollars. The experience was marred only by the unavailability of cerveza on May Day.

IT'S STRANGE THAT COOKING OVER mesquite has come to be associated with fancy restaurants in both northern Mexico and the United States. The cooking style is a throwback to the early days of the vaqueros, or Mexican cowboys. In fact, I got a chance to eat with some South Texas vaqueros not long ago.

The town of Linn in the Lower Rio Grande Valley is about a five-hour drive from my home in Houston. As soon as I got out of the car at St. Anne's church, the

CABRITO AL PASTOR roasting over mesquite coals at Los Norteños restaurant, Matamoros

smell of mesquite smoke enveloped me. "Get used to it," said Melissa Guerra, "Your clothes will smell like mesquite for weeks." Guerra had invited me to be a judge at the 26th Annual Linn–San Manuel Vaquero Cook-Off. She had laughingly described the event as a bunch of Tejanos out behind a church in the middle of nowhere and cooking over campfires.

South Texas cookbook author Melissa Guerra was raised on the nearby McAllen Ranch and her ancestors have been raising cattle in South Texas for eight generations. Wherever I looked, there were guys in straw cowboy hats and oversize sombreros building fires on the ground. Guerra's husband and the rest of the San Vincente Ranch cook-off team were busy making beans and boiling corn on the cob in giant iron pots. They were burning mesquite logs in a campfire set off by a circle of stones. The coals were shoveled into a four-foot-square steel box and a grate was set over the top. A tiny cabrito of about eight pounds was split whole and spread out ribs down over the coals.

When you mention Tex-Mex, most people think of chili con carne and combination plates. That's the stuff that was first marketed to Anglos under the banner of "Mexican food" in the mid-1800s. In the 1970s, an American obsession with authentic Mexican pushed old-fashioned Tex-Mex aside. And in the 1980s, mesquite-grilled fajitas and frozen margaritas sparked a Tex-Mex revival that also helped to fuel the explosive growth of backyard barbecue.

MESQUITE

Mesquite grilling was a plot by Texas ranchers to get a bunch of Californians to clear their rangeland for free—or so went the joke that made the rounds in West Texas back when fajitas first popularized the flavor of mesquite smoke.

Southwestern cuisine embellished the border cooking style, and mesquite-grilled steaks and chops became a distinctive part of the menu. Mesquite-burning grills were installed in southwestern restaurants, in Tex-Mex fajita joints, and even in upscale Texas hamburger chains like Becks Prime in Houston. In 1979, Ranchmen's Manufacturing of Dallas, one of the few places to buy mesquite wood, had around a thousand customers. By 1984, the company had more than twelve thousand clients. Today there are hundreds of places to buy mesquite wood in Texas. In 2005, twelve and half million pounds of mesquite chunks were sold to consumers across the country.

Historically, mesquite grilling wasn't very common in Texas outside of the Lower Rio Grande Valley. There were very few mesquite trees—or any other kind of trees—in South and West Texas. Before the Civil War, these areas were covered with an ocean of prairie grass. Wildfires and the hooves of millions of buffalo kept the brush under control. The few trees that existed hugged the banks of rivers and streams. And the Comanches scared away any settlers.

Mesquite began its advance when the buffalo were killed off and the Comanches were moved to reservations. During the cattle drive era of the late 1800s, cattlemen flooded into the prairie lands with their herds. Overgrazing destroyed the prairie and before long the sea of grass became a thicket of thorny mesquite.

Today mesquite occupies fifty to sixty million acres in South and West Texas. The tree competes with other vegetation for scarce water; it has a taproot that can extend for over a hundred feet downward to reach the water table. It's a nuisance, and it's almost impossible to kill. A mesquite tree can regenerate itself from the smallest piece of root left in the ground.

Mesquite has been transplanted to other places where it has also become a problem. It was introduced to Hawaii in 1828, where it is called the *kiawe* tree. It's now one of the most common trees in much of Hawaii, which is why mesquite grilling is also very popular in the islands.

At least you don't have to feel guilty about grilling with the stuff. Burn all the mesquite you like; no one will fault you for destroying the rain forest.

But mesquite grilling wasn't new. It's actually a much older style of Tejano cuisine than cheese enchiladas and combination plates. This kind of cooking had been part of the Spanish cattle culture for centuries. Which is why I was delighted to accept Guerra's invitation to participate in a real vaquero cooking contest. It was a chance to see Tex-Mex cooking as it was done in the beginning.

ONLY TWENTY TEAMS ARE INVITED each year to the Linn–San Manuel Vaquero Cook-Off; it's sort of the Super Bowl of vaquero cook-offs, Guerra told me. But in truth, the annual gathering of Tejano ranchfolk is more of a charity event than a cooking contest. It is the primary fund-raiser for St. Anne's Catholic Church and the Linn–San Manuel elementary school and fire department.

While the chuck-wagon cook-offs common in other parts of the state celebrate Texas cowboy cooking, the Linn–San Manuel Cook-Off is a celebration of vaquero cooking. The vaqueros, as Mexican cowboys are known, have their own cooking traditions. They make a flatbread called *pan de campo* in their Dutch ovens instead of the biscuits that Anglo cowboys baked, and the vaqueros grill their meats. It was the kind of fuel they used in the old days that made the biggest difference in cowboy and vaquero cooking techniques.

Cowboys worked with cattle and cooked over campfires, so you'd think they'd be pretty good at grilling steaks. Wrong. "The cowboys didn't really do much grilling," chuck-wagon cooking expert Tom Perini told me. There weren't any trees in the vast prairies of the South Plains when the cattle drives took place. The cowboys made their campfires with dried "buffalo chips." Imagine the flavor of a steak grilled over burning buffalo dung. That's why cowboys fried steaks in skillets and cooked chilis, stews, and beans in covered Dutch ovens.

Here in the Lower Rio Grande Valley, a few miles from Mexico, mesquite trees have always been plentiful. As I learned in Matamoros and Monterrey, grilling or slow-cooking meat over mesquite coals is a northern Mexican tradition that goes back to the immigrant Spanish herders. In

COMPETITOR IN the 2008 Linn–San Manuel Vaquero Cook-Off

northern Mexico, a kid goat is classically spread on a steel cross and rotated over the mesquite coals, in a preparation called *cabrito al pastor* ("in the style of the shepherd").

Like a lot of backyard barbecuers, I often use mesquite charcoal or mesquite wood for grilling because it imparts a lot of flavor in a short amount of time. But I avoid using it in my barbecue pit because the high level of resin imparts a nasty diesel fuel flavor to long-cooked meats.

The trick, as these vaqueros were demonstrating, is to burn the mesquite wood down and then cook over the hot coals. Using this technique, the flavor of the wood smoke is tamed from overwhelming to pleasantly bold.

VAQUERO COOK-OFF
fare: (clockwise) corn
on the cob with chile,
pan de campo, chile
pequin salsa in a
molcajete, bowl of
carne guisada, cabrito
taco, and short ribs

Mesquite wood and tiny wild chile pequíns (see page 232) are the two things that make the vaquero cooking of the Lower Rio Grande Valley unique—and both of them are free, a cook-off competitor told me as I strolled around observing the cooking. Some of the competitors used commercial seasoning blends from Bolner's Fiesta spices (see page 20). Some said they started with commercial seasoning blends and then doctored them with their own additions. One team had brought along an entire chile pequín bush.

Cabrito is one of the categories I was selected to judge at the Linn–San Manuel Cook-Off. The categories were fajitas, chili, *carne guisada* (stewed meat), frijoles, pan de campo, beef ribs, pork ribs, cabrito, and an open category. There were a dozen cabrito entries and each of the tiny baby goats had been splayed and cooked over mesquite coals for several hours with various seasonings. It was a difficult contest to judge.

The outer skin of the kid goats was hardened, but underneath the meat was very soft; some of the samples were juicier than others. In the top-ranked entries, the long strings of meat that carved away from the shoulder area were moist and milky white. But it was the meat from the riñonada—the area around the kidney—that melted in your mouth and sent your eyes rolling back in your head before you begged for more. One of the lady judges had wisely brought a large shopping bag, which she filled with leftovers when the judging was over.

In the open category, one contestant studded a whole seven-bone prime rib roast with garlic and slow-cooked it over mesquite coals. There were also quite a few pork rib racks cooking over coals.

In the ranch lands along the border and in the desert of northern Mexico, the grilling tradition has always been strong. Barbecuing over hot coals in open pits with no coverings to retain the smoke was the original technique in the old South and throughout Texas a century ago. It's the technique that Lyndon Johnson's barbecue caterer, Walter Jetton, swore by and it's still used today for whole-hog barbecue in the Carolinas and at such Texas barbecue joints as Cooper's in Llano. The only difference between mesquite grilling and open-pit barbecue is the duration.

Mesquite grilling in your backyard is easy for small quick-cooking cuts. You start with mesquite wood and burn it down until only coals remain—then start cooking. For larger cuts, you need a fire that's separate from the grill. When your heat gets low, you burn some more mesquite and then put the coals into the grill; you can use a chimney starter if you're using a small grill.

Mesquite grilling is the pride of the Tex-Mex tradition, but it's not the only grilling method in Texas or Mexico. I happened upon one team at the Linn–San Manuel Cook-Off using Kingsford charcoal briquettes instead of mesquite coals. When I asked about it, the guy who was stoking the fire told me with a smile: "Charcoal is a lot easier."

THE AVERAGE CITIZENS OF THE BORder region don't eat a lot of cabrito and they don't cook with mesquite. Street food is prepared on propane grills and flat tops and it's the most popular way to grab a quick snack. There's an incredible array of choices. In Texas, there are taco trucks, taco trailers, *carnicerias* (butcher shops that sell meals), taquerias, and *ostionerias* (oyster bars). In northern Mexico, torta shops sell Mexican sandwiches and taco stands are everywhere. Fruit vendors sell paper cones of pineapple or melon chunks sprinkled with powdered chile and cold fruit-flavored *aguas frescas*.

In Matamoros, I visited the civic-sponsored outdoor food stalls of Plaza Allende. On two sides of the lovely urban square, there were long rows of identical wooden kiosks, each housing a tiny fast-food operation. Inside each, the *taquero*, as the proprietor of a taco stand is known, cooked on a propane-fueled grill.

Some of the stalls turned out tacos, some made quesadillas, and some specialized in tortas. Others offered tacos al pastor made from the revolving cones of pork topped with pineapple cooking on vertical roasters (see page 170).

I was especially intrigued by the stalls that had a gas grill and a flat top side by side. The proprietors were grilling meat on the grate of the gas grill and at the same time caramelizing onions and peppers, heating tortillas, and toasting buns on the flat top.

MAKING FLOUR tortillas on a flat top

and all that labor-intensive shoveling of coals. But eventually I started to realize that while gas grills were ubiquitous, they were often only the last stage in a multipart cooking process.

The guy selling tacos al pastor was a good example. The pork was actually slow-cooking on the vertical roaster. The grill was only used in the final step of making the tacos. It's the same thing with taco trucks in the United States. The guy selling *barbacoa* tacos wasn't slow-cooking cow heads on the flat top where he was making tacos; the barbacoa was prepared in advance as were the *asados*, guisadas, and many of the other meats.

To test recipes for this book, I bought a gas grill and a "big ugly barrel," a fifty-five-gallon drum turned on its side and cut in half. I lined these up beside the large offset barbecue smoker I have been using for the last twenty years.

This might sound like a lot of outdoor cooking equipment, but if you can believe statistics, I am probably fairly average. The rise in the sales of gas grills might lead you to believe that they are replacing charcoal grills. But the rise in the sale of charcoal would seem to signal an entirely different picture. More and more Americans own both kinds of grills and use them side by side. And the continued rise in the sales of wood chips and chunks also indicates that lots of people want to get smoky flavors from the grill.

It seemed like the ideal combination of cooking surfaces for a modern taquero.

Slow cooking over mesquite is a lovely old-fashioned ideal, but modern Mexican street food is cooked on a gas grill or a propane-fired flat top. I would see the same sort of setup again and again at street vendors' stalls in Mexico and at taco trucks in the United States.

It seemed like evolution. The easy and convenient gas grill and flat top had replaced the primitive mesquite- and charcoal-burning contraptions

The best taqueros use all kinds of equipment. Every couple of days, they slow-cook meats over mesquite or braise or stew them. And then they use these cooked-in-advance ingredients to make tacos to order on the gas grill. It's a very clever strategy.

Some of the recipes in this book can be cooked on any kind of grill. Some call for specific equipment. But if you happen to have both a gas grill and a large covered charcoal grill, you can borrow the taqueros' technique.

Your charcoal grill imparts more flavor to your expensive steaks, roasts, and whole fish. And it's easier to avoid flare-ups with indirect cooking on a charcoal grill. But you can use your gas grill to make side dishes, caramelize onions and peppers, cook mushrooms, and prepare tacos, quesadillas, and tortas while you cook meat at the same time. And when you're in a hurry, you can always just use the gas grill to make chops, hot dogs, *hamburguesas*, shrimp dishes, and other quick fare.

There is no right way or wrong way to grill Tex-Mex style, as long as the food tastes great. No matter if your grill burns mesquite logs, charcoal, or propane, you can find a Tex-Mex recipe that fits the equipment. Here're a few tips on using some of the most common grills:

Grills

Covered Charcoal Grills

PIONEERED BY WEBER, THIS IS THE great American grill. The cover retains heat and smoke and controls airflow to prevent flare-ups. Many companies make good covered charcoal grills these days, but be sure you get one with vents on the top and bottom to control the heat and with two grates—one for food and one for the coals.

Covered charcoal grills range in size from tiny tabletop models to the enormous Weber Ranch Kettle, a thousand-dollar charcoal grill with a grate that's three feet across. A medium-size Weber should cost under one hundred dollars, and an Old Smokey can be found for around fifty. The optional hinged grills that you can lift to add more wood or coals during the cooking process are highly recommended. Buy the charcoal containers that confine the coals and keep the fire from spreading, too.

Barrel Grills (also known as Ugly Drums, Big Ugly Barrels, or Texas Hibachis)

A BARREL SMOKER IS A FIFTY-FIVE-gallon metal drum turned on its side, sawed in half, and fitted with a chimney, legs, and handles. They sell for under a hundred dollars and can be found outside many grocery stores in Texas. Plans for welding them are also available online.

A barrel smoker gives you lots of grill capacity and enough headroom (vertical clearance) for a turkey or cow head. There is also plenty of room underneath to burn wood, or at least to throw a few logs onto a charcoal fire. If you get two or three years out of a barrel smoker, you're doing fine; think of it as a disposable grill. The tops never close evenly, the grills burn through, and sooner or later the barrel rusts out or the welds break.

But don't write them off; some people think the Texas hibachi is the perfect grill. I added an extra grate on the bottom of my barrel to keep the coals off the floor and improve the airflow. You can also drill holes for more air. (There are lots of plans for customizing barrel grills on the Internet, including directions for construction of a "double barrel.")

Offset Smokers

THE FIREBOX AND GRILL ARE ON ONE side, and a separate smoke chamber big enough to hold a brisket, five pounds of sausage, and a couple of chickens is on the other side. The smoke chamber has a built-in thermometer on top, and there's a drain plug for cleaning on the bottom. The drawback for grilling is that the grill area is relatively small. Offset grills start around six hundred fifty dollars.

Gas Grills

GAS GRILLS ARE POWERED BY PRO-pane tanks or a natural gas line and they range in price from under two hundred dollars to tens of thousands of dollars. These grills use porcelain or lava rock briquettes or some sort of steel surface to convert gas to radiant heat. They feature electronic ignition for easy lighting. Temperature controls allow heat adjustment from low for roasts and turkeys, to high for steaks, chops, and hamburgers. The cooking surface on gas grills ranges in size from around 150 square inches to more than 500 square inches.

PLAZA ALLENDE
taquero stalls, Matamoros

The biggest problems with gas grills come from flare-ups. Cooking fatty food directly over the gas flames causes the food to catch on fire. Some gas grills are designed to cook using indirect heat only, preventing such mishaps, but they don't sear the meat or give you the desired grill marks. Flavor-wise, there isn't much difference between cooking with indirect heat on a gas grill and putting the food in the oven.

Gas grills excel for making a quick dinner as long as you keep your eye out for flare-ups. If your steak or burger catches fire, turn down the heat and move the meat to a cooler spot on the grill to finish cooking at a slower rate.

If you are buying a new gas grill, consider getting one that allows you to replace one side of the grill grate with a flat top.

Flat Tops and *Comals*

THE BEST PIECE OF EQUIPMENT YOU can add to your backyard barbecue arsenal is a flat top, comal, or a griddle. It will save you the bother of trying to cook in the backyard and on top of the kitchen stove at the same time.

You can stick a frying pan or a flat Mexican pan called a *comal* on top of the grate of your gas or charcoal grill. A comal is usually made of black cast iron. It looks like a cast-iron skillet without any sides. The reason it doesn't have sides is so you can flip a stack of tortillas on it without burning your fingers. A cast-iron skillet or comal will do fine for the recipes in this book—as long as you don't try to cook too many things at the same time.

Once you begin to enjoy the advantages of having a comal handy, you may start looking at griddle attachments you can buy to fit on your grill. Griddle attachments (or flat tops) will give you a larger surface on which to fry bacon, heat tortillas, and caramelize onions all at the same time. In fact, they will allow you to do anything a short-order cook can do.

The ultimate in outdoor griddles is the kind that replaces one of the grates on a gas grill. Once you have one of these versatile flat tops, it's hard to remember how you did without it.

Brick and Masonry Pits

OF COURSE, A PERMANENT OUTDOOR smoker made of brick or cinder block is the ultimate in barbecue pits—providing it's properly designed. If you are going to have somebody build one for you, make sure they start with plans that provide for a controllable airflow and variable grill height.

Consider the Argentine asado hut design. This kind of grill is built into an outbuilding with a roof for inclement weather. The grill grates can be raised and lowered over the fire by use of a mechanical crank. The grill elements are V-shaped metal rods that catch grease and moisture and direct them into a grease receptacle. It may sound complicated, but you can find plans online.

COOKING ON a flat top in a Matamoros taqueria

Tools You'll Need

Tongs The long barbecue tongs don't handle heavy things very well. I like the short, spring-loaded kind you get at restaurant supply houses.

Spatula Any metal one will do.

Basting Mop Nylon brushes melt, and basting brushes are too dainty. The best idea is to find a little cotton mop—the kind used for washing dishes.

Wire Brush No, the black gunk stuck to the grill doesn't add flavor—not the good kind, anyway. Clean your grill with a wire brush every time you barbecue.

Poker A stout stick from the yard will do, but you need something to move hot coals.

Heavy-Duty Aluminum Foil Lots of the recipes in this book call for you to wrap the meat in foil. You'll need the heavy-gauge, extra-wide variety.

Drip Pans and Water Pans A drip pan is a container placed under the meat to keep the fat from falling in the fire and flaring up. It is usually filled with water or some other liquid (such as Lone Star beer). A water pan is a pan placed in the smoke chamber between the food and the fire for the purpose of keeping a high level of moisture in the smoke chamber so the meat doesn't dry out. In a water smoker, a pan filled with water placed between the meat and the fire serves both purposes at once.

If you are cooking a meat that dries out easily, such as turkey, a water pan is a great idea. If you are cooking meat that is fatty, you may need a drip pan to keep the fire from flaring up. You don't want to use a water pan while you're trying to get something crisp.

I use a little metal cake pan, but I have accepted the fact that it will never be clean enough to bake a cake in again.

Charcoal Starter Chimney A charcoal starter chimney is a cylindrical container with a grate in the middle and a fireproof handle on the outside. (Weber makes an extra-large one that suits me perfectly.) You fill the top of the container with charcoal, stuff some newspaper in the bottom, and light the paper. Within ten minutes or so, you have hot coals without using any starter fluid. Some people use paraffin in their chimney along with the newspaper, but you don't need it.

These chimneys became popular in California after the city of Los Angeles banned the use of charcoal starter fluid because it is an environmental menace. It's a culinary menace, too. If you're not careful, you end up with barbecue that smells like an oil refinery.

NOTE: Never put a lit chimney on a picnic table, deck, or other flammable surface.

Thermometers Most grills have a thermometer that can be read from the outside. If yours doesn't, you can also stick a candy thermometer through the vent of your smoker to keep track of the temperature inside.

You will also need an instant-read internal temperature thermometer to check the doneness of the meat. I used to use a probe thermometer/timer made by Polder. The probe was inserted into the meat, and a wire connected the probe to a digital readout outside the smoker that displayed the internal temperature of the meat. Unfortunately, I kept burning out the wires.

In gimmick-loving barbecue circles, the ultimate thermometer is the Remote-Check from Maverick. This thermometer comes with two internal temperature probes that have heat-proof wires leading to a transmitter that sits outside the barbecue. Two internal temperatures are beamed to a handheld remote that can be taken indoors so you can monitor both pieces of meat while you watch football. I used to have one, but the transmitter stopped working.

Now I use a portable internal temperature thermometer called a Taylor Weekend Warrior. It has a thin metal probe and a digital readout and

PUT THE hardwood beside the coals so it smolders

sells for under twenty dollars. When I lose it or break it, it won't be too big an investment to buy another one.

Choose any style you like, but don't try to do without. An internal-temperature meat thermometer is essential to know when your meat is properly cooked and to ensure food safety.

Fuels

Charcoal Lump hardwood charcoal is the irregular kind that's not made into briquettes. It burns hot and is great for steaks and chops. Lump mesquite charcoal imparts a great flavor, but be forewarned about its explosive tendencies: it pops, sparks, and sends hot charcoal pieces flying around as it burns. Don't try starting it in a chimney starter. You are better off to use Kingsford, or any other standard brand of pure charcoal briquette, to start your fire. Then you can add mesquite wood or mesquite lump charcoal a little at a time. Avoid cheap composite charcoals, including the composite mesquite charcoal, which contain paraffin or petroleum by-products; you're better off with mesquite wood or mesquite chips or chunks.

Wood Mesquite is very resinous and burns hot. Grilling steaks, chops, or burgers over a mesquite fire is fine, but longer cooking with mesquite requires some adjustments. Burn the mesquite down first and then cook over the embers.

The flavor of mesquite is not for everyone and even if you love it, it's nice to use other woods for a change of pace. If you have hickory, maple, alder, cherry, apple, oak, pecan, walnut, or some other hardwood in your yard, you can cut up a few logs or stout sticks and use them for grilling.

Starting a Fire

START WITH TWENTY-FIVE BRIQUETTES. As soon as you see flames coming out of the top of the chimney, dump the charcoal into the firebox or grate of your smoker. (If you forget to dump the charcoal, the chimney will quickly burn up all your fuel, and you'll have to start over.) You can start adding wood as soon as you dump the coals. If you are using lighter fluid, be sure to wait until the coals are white before you start cooking so you don't get any lighter fluid taste.

Spread the coals out on the lower grate. One layer is adequate for around an hour of cooking time. For a larger grill or a hotter temperature, add about twenty-five more briquettes once you get the first batch lit. This will bring the temperature up to about 350°F very quickly. The bigger the pile of charcoal you light, the hotter the fire will burn.

To control the heat level, spread out the coals and close down the dampers to reduce the heat and drop the temperature. Then open the dampers a little at a time to increase the ventilation rate and raise the temperature to the desired level.

When you add wood chunks or logs to a charcoal fire, add them to the side of the fire so that they smolder slowly, rather than on top of the charcoal, where they will burn quickly.

For long-cooking meats, add a second layer of wood or charcoal before the first layer burns out.

Direct and Indirect Heat Setups

COOKING OVER DIRECT HEAT

To set up a grill for cooking over direct heat, spread hot coals evenly across the firebox, leaving a little  area empty. Put the meat on a grill as far as possible above the coals. This is fine for steaks, chops, and burgers, but you will need to be sure to keep them from flaring up. If you get a flare-up, move the flaming meat above the area of the firebox where there aren't any coals.

COOKING OVER INDIRECT HEAT

You can set up almost any grill for indirect cooking by putting the fire on one side of the unit and the meat on the other. A drip pan is often positioned under the meat to prevent flare-ups.

 If you have split logs, you can lay a piece of wood across the firebox to divide the area in half and then pour hot charcoal briquettes on one side of it. The charcoal will cause the log to smolder, creating plenty of smoke. Then put the meat over the empty half of the grate for indirect cooking.

Covered Grills

Light the charcoal in a starter chimney. Arrange the coals on one side of the fire grate or fire pan or in the two Weber charcoal pans or by using a log as a divider. Use a drip pan filled with water if possible. After browning directly over the coals, slow-cook the meat over the water pan on the side of the grill away from the coals. Control the temperature with the top air vent over the meat and the bottom air vent under the fire, and close the other vents. Refuel as necessary.

Barrel Grills (Ugly Drums, Big Ugly Barrels, or Texas Hibachis)

You can also use a barrel smoker for direct or indirect cooking. For direct cooking, light a fire in one end of the smoker and spread the coals out as needed. Put the meat over the fire.

When using indirect heat, light a fire in one end of the smoker only. You can move the meat closer or farther away to maintain a good cooking temperature. The part of the meat facing the fire will be the hottest, so rotate it to keep the cooking even. Don't overload the grill with meat. Control the fire by opening and closing the chimney damper and fuel door to raise and lower the ventilation rate. Stick an oven thermometer inside for accuracy.

How to Tell When It's Done

THE USDA RECOMMENDS AN INTERNAL temperature of 185°F for chicken. Commercial chicken is submerged in a water bath after it is killed to cool it down for processing, and it absorbs some of the water. The water spreads the germs from one chicken to another. To prevent salmonella poisoning, chicken processors recommend you cook their chicken to 185°F.

In an experiment on my grill, it took more than five and a half hours to get a whole chicken to 185°F, at which point it was black as a cinder. When I wiggled the leg, the bone came all the way out. When I carved the bird, the breast was dry. For my own tastes, I am willing to take a gamble—but not with commercial chicken.

Instead of burning my chicken to kill salmonella, I buy "smart chickens"—free-range chickens that are given no antibiotics, animal feed, or growth hormones. Instead, they are raised on grains grown without pesticides, herbicides, fungicides, and chemical fertilizers. Most important, these chickens are individually air cooled—not immersed in a germ-laden cold-water bath en masse. I cook this chicken to around 170°F, at which point it passes the leg-wiggling and knife-point insertion tests (the leg moves freely and the juices run clear when you insert a knife tip in the thickest part of the thigh).

I don't follow all the USDA guidelines for other meats, either. Because of the scandals involving contaminated ground beef a few years ago, Bruce

WHAT AM I DOING WRONG?

Here are the four most common mistakes people make while grilling.

TOO HOT You can burn anything if you use too much charcoal. Twenty-five briquettes is plenty for quick-cooking meats like steaks or burgers. For chicken, whole fish, and thicker cuts like pork or tri-tip roast, you need to use a first layer of briquettes spread thin to create a wide area of medium to low heat, followed by a second fueling.

Start with only one layer of coals and spread them so they barely touch each other under the area covered by the meat being grilled. In covered grills, a few coals can be added after an hour of cooking in a second layer. Start the air vents at half open and then adjust to three-fourths to fully open during the latter part of the grilling. On a gas grill, light just one set of burners, adjust to medium, and after browning quickly, cook the meat away from the flame.

TOO FAST When your steak flares up, catches fire, and turns black, you may decide it's time to take it off the grill. Surely it's overdone, right? No—not if the internal temperature is still only 120°F. Steak and chops that are eaten medium-rare take roughly seven minutes a side or fifteen minutes on the grill and should register at least 135°F. Burgers take fifteen to twenty minutes to reach an internal temperature of 160°F.

Chicken halves, whole fish, and roasts require a grilling time of at least one and a half hours under perfect conditions. If the fire dies down too much and has to be revived, the cooking time can easily stretch to two hours or more. To avoid bad decisions, use an internal-temperature thermometer—not your hunger level—to determine doneness.

TOO CLOSE Using indirect heat on covered grills, five to ten inches between the fire and grill rack is adequate, because the heat is easier to control. With gas grills and open-top grills, the greater the distance from the fire the better.

TOO BLACK Barbecue sauces contain tomatoes, ketchup, and sweet ingredients that burn and turn black during cooking. Oil and vinegar–based mop sauces are fine for basting during the cooking process, but not barbecue sauce. Wait until the food is nearly done and then apply sweet barbecue sauce or other glazes and cook just until they bubble and set; don't walk away and let them burn.

GEBHARDT EAGLE Chili Powder was registered as a trademark in 1899

Aidells' *Complete Meat Cookbook* explains, the USDA published recommended doneness temperatures for all varieties of meat that were ten to fifteen degrees higher than those used by most restaurants.

In her cookbook *Roasting*, Barbara Kafka notes, "If I cooked beef and lamb to the recommended temperatures, I would never produce rare meat again." In this book, I provide both a lower temperature at which to begin testing for doneness when you are willing to risk it, and the higher USDA recommended temperature, for those times when you are concerned with safety.

At Texas A&M, I met a meat scientist who summed up the subject nicely. "When I'm cooking a burger for myself, I start with top-quality meat and cook it medium-rare, maybe 140°F—but that's a calculated risk that I choose to take. When I am cooking burgers for children, I cook them to the USDA's recommended 160°F. And you can be darn sure I have a thermometer in my hand."

Grill Seasonings

CHILE AND CUMIN ARE THE HEART OF the Tex-Mex flavor signature. The liberal use of cumin came with immigrants from the Canary Islands in the 1700s. The chiles of the *Capsicum annum* species are indigenous to North America and have been used in cooking here for thousands of years. (For identification, see Chile Peppers on page 230.)

Chili powders, such as Gebhardt Chili Powder or Adams Chili Powder, are spice blends containing powdered ancho chiles, cumin, garlic, oregano, and other ingredients. Chili powder is a fine ingredient, but if you want to make your own spice blends, it's best to start out with pure powdered chiles.

The traditional powdered chile in West Texas and New Mexico is the dried and pulverized New Mexican red chile. You can order it online or buy it in a specialty store. Grinding your own chile powders isn't very hard with a spice grinder or coffee grinder. (See the instructions on page 233.) But several spice companies, including McCormick and Adams, now sell powdered chiles.

The recipes in this book also call for paprika, which is a Central European powdered chile. While both sweet and hot paprikas are available, we'll assume you're using sweet paprika. *Pimentón*, or smoked paprika, is a wonderful product that gives food a smoky barbecued flavor. The imported versions are excellent, but domestic spice companies are now selling smoked paprika as well.

Commercial Blends
Many Tex-Mex grillers start off with a commercial spice blend. Some use them straight and some doctor them up. Here are few favorites:

ADAMS EXTRACT AND SPICE (ADAMSEXTRACT.COM)
Founded as a vanilla extractor in 1888 in Michigan, Adams has been headquartered in Texas since 1905. The company expanded into the spice market in the 1960s with a popular chili powder. Now headquartered in Gonzales, Texas, the company specializes in spice blends for the Tex-Mex market. Pinto Bean Seasoning and Menudo Seasoning are new blends from the oldest spice company in Texas.

Under the new Adams Reserve label, you'll also find everything you need to make your own blends at home. The line includes ancho chile powder, chipotle powder, whole dried chile pequíns, New Mexican chile powder, New Mexican green chile flakes, granulated jalapeño, and cracked black pepper and mesquite-smoked black pepper.

FIESTA (FIESTASPICES.COM)
Fajita Seasoning and Brisket Rub are categories that were popularized by Bolner's Fiesta Products in San Antonio, a family-owned company that has been in the business since 1955 and remains a favorite in South Texas. The company's pork rub, chicken rub, rib rub, and wild game rub are very popular. Fiesta also sells dried chiles and powdered chiles by mail order, in case you can't find them in your grocery store.

TEXJOY (TEXJOY.COM)
Steak Seasoning and Barbecue Seasoning are the old favorite seasoning blends from TexJoy, the spice division of the Texas Coffee Company, a family-owned company that was founded in Beaumont in 1921. TexJoy now makes their steak seasoning in regular, spicy, and Worcestershire varieties. Their products are found mainly in the Houston and Beaumont area.

TEXAS SPICE COMPANY (TEXAS-SPICE.NET)
A relative newcomer, Texas Spice has been selling powdered chiles and seasoning blends for the barbecue and grill since 1985. The company is located in Round Rock, and its products are best known in the Austin area. Texas Spice Company specializes in custom blending for wholesalers and the many marketers of private-label spice blends.

Homemade Spice Blends
So with all of these spice blends on the market, why bother making your own? Look at the label of the spice blend you're about to buy. Does it contain anything you're trying to avoid, like MSG or lots of salt? You'll notice that most spice blends are dominated by a few cheap ingredients like onion and garlic powder with salt and pepper. If you have those things at home, why pay to get more of them in a jar?

But the best reason to make your own spice blend is because you can use flavorful but expensive herbs you like, such as coriander and thyme, in the quantity you choose. You can also use your own homemade ground chiles to ensure fresh, hot flavors. For more about grinding your own chile powder, see page 233.

Here are a few recipes to get you started.

Tex-Mex Grill Blend

MAKES ABOUT 1 CUP

THIS ALL-PURPOSE GRILL SEASONING WORKS ON JUST ABOUT anything.

- 4 tablespoons sea salt
- 3 tablespoons powdered chile of your choice
- 2 tablespoons dried granulated garlic
- 2 tablespoons coarsely ground black pepper
- 1 tablespoon ground thyme
- 1 teaspoon ground coriander
- 1 teaspoon ground cumin

Combine all of the ingredients in a small bowl, blending well to evenly distribute the spices. Be sure to break up any chunks that appear. Store the blend in a spice jar or baby food container. Shake or stir again before each use.

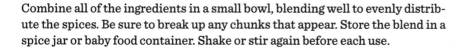

Tejano Pork Rub

MAKES ABOUT ½ CUP

ANCHO CHILE AND BROWN SUGAR COMBINE BEAUTIFULLY IN this pork seasoning blend.

- 1 tablespoon brown sugar
- 2 tablespoons garlic powder
- 2 teaspoons sea salt
- 2 teaspoons cracked black pepper
- 2 teaspoons powdered ancho chile
- 1 teaspoon ground thyme
- 1 teaspoon ground Mexican oregano

Combine all of the ingredients in a small bowl, blending well to evenly distribute the spices. Be sure to break up any chunks that appear. Store the blend in a spice jar or baby food container. Shake or stir again before each use.

Chile Paste

YOU CAN VARY THE DRIED CHILES IF YOU WANT TO MAKE DIF-ferent kinds of chile pastes. Use this as a base for all kinds of sauces.

Dried chiles, such as anchos, New Mexican red chiles, or dried chipotles

Rinse the chiles to remove any dust or dirt. Slit each one with a sharp knife and remove and discard the seeds and stem. Place the peppers in a large saucepan and cover with water. Bring to a boil over high heat, reduce the heat, and allow the peppers to soften in the simmering water for 15 minutes. Pour the pepper mixture and ½ cup or so of the cooking liquid into the container of a blender. Cover and start blending on low speed, increasing to high speed as the puree becomes combined.

Chile Butter

MAKES EIGHT 1-OUNCE PORTIONS

ANCHO BUTTER IS MY FAVORITE VARIETY, BUT GUAJILLO chiles make a wonderful chile butter, too. Try a decorative medallion of chile butter on a grilled steak. It's indispensable for grilled corn on the cob.

1 dried chile, stemmed, seeded, and softened in hot water
2 cloves garlic, minced
1 cup (2 sticks) butter, softened
Sea salt

VARIATION
To make herb butter, use 4 tablespoons minced cilantro or parsley instead of the chile.

Place the softened chile, garlic, butter, and salt to taste in a mixer fitted with the paddle attachment and beat at medium speed until light and fluffy. Put the butter mixture in the refrigerator for an hour to allow the flavors to develop.

Remove the butter mixture from the bowl with a rubber spatula and place on a length of foil. Roll the mixture into a 1½-inch-wide log, squeezing to remove any air pockets and rolling to shape the cylinder evenly. Wrap tightly in the foil and freeze until ready for use.

For steaks, cut the butter into disks (don't try to unwrap it, just cut through the foil and then remove the foil). Put a cold disk of flavored butter on top of a sizzling steak. For grilled corn and other uses, let a portion of the chile butter thaw and spread as needed.

Chile butter will keep in the freezer for several months.

CORN ON the cob on sale at the vaquero cook-off

Red Rub

MAKES ABOUT ¾ CUP

THIS IS AN EXCELLENT RUB ON CHICKEN OR GAME BIRDS, BUT IT works well on fish and shrimp, too.

- 2 tablespoons granulated garlic
- 1 tablespoon powdered red chile
- 3 tablespoons paprika (or smoked paprika, see page 20)
- 1 tablespoon sea salt
- 1 tablespoon brown sugar
- 1 tablespoon granulated onion
- 1 teaspoon ground cumin
- ½ teaspoon ground cinnamon

Combine all of the ingredients in a small bowl, blending well to evenly distribute the spices. Be sure to break up any chunks that appear. Store the blend in a spice jar or baby food container. Shake or stir again before each use.

Perini Ranch Rib-Eye Rub

MAKES ABOUT ½ CUP, ENOUGH FOR 3 OR 4 LARGE STEAKS

TOM PERINI OWNS A RANCH IN BUFFALO GAP OUTSIDE OF Abilene with a steak house on it. He is also one of the state's foremost authorities on chuck-wagon cooking. His idea here was to imitate the crusty exterior of a chicken-fried steak by adding a little flour to the rub.

- 2 teaspoons flour
- 2 teaspoons salt
- 3 tablespoons coarsely ground black pepper
- ½ teaspoon ground Mexican oregano
- 4 teaspoons garlic powder

Combine the ingredients, mixing well. Store in a tightly sealed glass or plastic container. Shake before each use to remix the ingredients. Rub the blend into your steaks, then refrigerate for at least 15 minutes before cooking.

Coffee-Chipotle BBQ Sauce

MAKES ABOUT 4 CUPS

COWBOY COOKS NEVER THREW AWAY THE LEFTOVER BREAKFAST
coffee; they recycled it into recipes like this one.

1 tablespoon oil
2 cups diced yellow onion
7 cloves garlic, minced
1 cup ketchup
1 cup chipotle chile paste (see page 22)
½ cup strong coffee
½ cup Worcestershire sauce
⅓ cup packed brown sugar
¼ cup cider vinegar
¼ cup freshly squeezed lemon juice
1½ tablespoons Dijon mustard
2 teaspoons kosher salt

In a large, heavy saucepan, heat the oil over medium heat and add the onion
and garlic. Sauté until they begin to wilt. Add the ketchup and chile paste and
sauté for 4 minutes. Add all of the remaining ingredients, stir, and simmer gently for 30 to 40 minutes. As the sauce thickens, stir more often so it does not
scorch. Remove the sauce from the heat and cool. Place in a blender and puree.
Store in a clean container in the refrigerator for up to 2 weeks.

Tex-Maui BBQ Sauce

MAKES ABOUT 5 CUPS

YOU MIGHT BE SURPRISED TO LEARN THAT LOTS OF TEX-MEX cooks use soy sauce and other Asian ingredients in their cooking. This pineapple-based barbecue sauce goes well with pork, chicken, and shrimp. It was inspired by Tex-Mex legend Matt Martinez Jr. (see page 41) and his soy-based sauces.

2 cups pineapple juice
¼ cup rice wine vinegar
½ cup soy sauce
½ teaspoon salt
1¼ cups ketchup
1 tablespoon Dijon mustard
1 cup minced onion
½ teaspoon Chinese five-spice powder
1½ tablespoons Sriracha hot sauce
3 tablespoons hoisin sauce
1 lemon, sliced thin and seeded
2 tablespoons garlic-ginger paste (see Note)

Combine all ingredients in a saucepan and simmer until the onions and lemon are soft. Strain and serve immediately, or store in the refrigerator in a sealed container for up to 3 weeks.

NOTE: You can find garlic-ginger paste in Asian food stores or substitute an equal amount of fresh minced garlic and fresh minced ginger.

Ancho–Root Beer BBQ Sauce

MAKES ABOUT 4 CUPS

USE A STRONG ROOT BEER THAT'S SWEETENED WITH CANE sugar for this recipe. This stuff tastes great on chicken wings; see the recipe on page 118.

3 ancho chiles
3 cups good-quality root beer
1 cup cider vinegar
1 cup brown sugar
½ cup ketchup
1 tablespoon Worcestershire sauce
1 tablespoon salt or to taste
Freshly ground black pepper
8 tablespoons (1 stick) butter
1 onion, chopped
2 cloves garlic, minced

Rinse the outside of the anchos, then remove the seeds and stems and soak in hot water for 20 or 30 minutes until soft. Puree the chiles and a little of the soaking water in a blender. Set aside.

Combine the root beer, vinegar, brown sugar, ketchup, Worcestershire, salt, and pepper to taste in a large saucepan and simmer until the sugar is dissolved.

In a small skillet over medium heat, melt the butter and sauté the onion for 5 minutes. Add the garlic and sauté for 5 more minutes, or until the onion and garlic are softened. Add the chile puree and simmer for 5 minutes more. Add to the root beer mixture in the saucepan and stir to combine. Bring to a boil, then reduce the heat and simmer until slightly thickened. Allow to cool. Process in batches in the blender until smooth. Serve immediately or store in the refrigerator in a sealed container for up to 3 weeks.

THE ORIGINAL Cadillac
Bar in Nuevo Laredo
opened in 1926

CHAPTER 2

FROZEN MARGARITAS AND THE CADILLAC BAR

I N 1983, A HUGELY PROFITABLE 4,400-SQUARE-FOOT BAR and grill in San Francisco called the Cadillac Bar started a new restaurant genre. There was a giant mesquite grill along one wall and you could smell grilled meat and mesquite smoke from way down the street. It was named after the original Cadillac Bar in Nuevo Laredo, Mexico, and was decorated with beer signs and memorabilia collected in the border towns along the Rio Grande. As a former Austinite living in San Francisco in the 1980s, I treated the Cadillac as my home away from home.

The original Cadillac Bar was opened in 1926, by a New Orleans waiter named Mayo Bessan. He moved to Nuevo Laredo, bought a bar called the Caballo Blanco, and changed the name to the Cadillac Bar. He chose the name because it sounded rich and because his target market was Texas. The bar specialized in the trendy drink of the era, the Ramos Gin Fizz.

"Big Daddy" Bessan didn't know anything about Mexican food and he never learned Spanish. He didn't need to. Thanks to Prohibition, droves of well-heeled Americans were crossing the border in search of refreshments and a night on the town. The Cadillac became their preferred destination. The menu was in English and the prices were in dollars. Entrees included Italian spaghetti with meatballs, New Orleans shrimp Creole, crab Newburg, and chicken mole Mexicana. The kitchen also offered broiled steaks, veal chops, lobster, and frog legs. And then there was the standard Mexican dinner combo plate.

The wild success of Nuevo Laredo's Cadillac Bar inspired similar ventures in other border towns. Posh restaurants and night clubs on the other side included the Kentucky Club in Juárez, the Drive-In in Matamoros, and the Victory Club in Piedras Negras. They all catered to Americans crossing the border from Texas.

Bessan's daughter Wanda and her husband, Porter Garner Jr., took over when Bessan retired and the Garners operated the Cadillac Bar until the late 1970s, when they turned the keys over to the employees and walked away. They could see the handwriting on the wall: there would soon be little reason to go to Mexican border-town bars like the Cadillac.

It was in 1970 that the "liquor by the drink" amendment passed the Texas legislature. It's hard to believe, but cocktails weren't available in Texas restaurants at the time. Shortly after the law changed, new Tex-Mex restaurants with expansive bars began to pop up, and they were modeled after the famous border-town cantinas.

The Cadillac Bar, and the enticing blend of luxury, liquor, and south-of-the-border dining that it represented, became the model for a new style of restaurant, the contemporary Tex-Mex bar and grill. A Cadillac Bar in San Antonio opened in 1973. The Landry's restaurant group now operates a Cadillac Bar in Houston and another one in Kemah.

CADILLAC MANAGER
and bartenders with
dinner specials and
cocktails

But it was the San Francisco Cadillac, with its giant mesquite grill and Mexican decorations, that became the most famous. Frozen margaritas and mesquite-grilled fajitas were the most popular order at the San Francisco restaurant. Large orders like mesquite-grilled cabrito and seafood platters that fed five or six people were among the other favorite dishes.

The owners of the San Francisco Cadillac Bar described their cooking as authentic Mexican and bragged that many of the recipes came from the namesake restaurant in Nuevo Laredo. They neglected to mention that Mayo Bessan was from New Orleans and that the Cadillac Bar was never an authentic Mexican restaurant. The frozen margaritas and grilled fajitas they were serving were pure Tex-Mex. But the mistaken belief among consumers that this was authentic Mexican fare turned out to be a godsend for Tex-Mex restaurant owners.

I N 1972, A HUGELY INFLUENTIAL COOKbook called *The Cuisines of Mexico* by Diana Kennedy trashed the "mixed plates" that were sold as Mexican food north of the border. Kennedy's dim view of Tex-Mex was endorsed by her friend Craig Claiborne at the *New York Times*. Knowledgeable food lovers began to demand authentic Mexican cooking and to snub Tex-Mex. And as a result, countless Mexican-American families watched their restaurants go out of business.

Sizzling fajitas and frozen margaritas saved the day. They also changed the architecture. Vintage Tex-Mex restaurants didn't have bars, but from the 1970s on, the bar became the center of nearly every Tex-Mex restaurant that wasn't in a dry county. Along with the new focus on the bar came a different atmosphere.

Customers had once gone to mom-and-pop Tex-Mex diners to enjoy a combo platter and depart, but the festive new cantinas were designed to be hangouts. Many featured outdoor seating on patios or decks. The gang who went to get a drink after work now included more women and they favored the new Tex-Mex bar and grill over male-dominated bars and taverns. Happy-hour margarita drinkers made communal cocktail snacks or botanas like nachos and

THE INVENTION OF THE FROZEN MARGARITA

The original margarita machine, a slightly altered frozen custard dispenser, is now in the Smithsonian Institution. Mariano Martinez, the man who made frozen margaritas famous, donated it to the museum some years ago.

In 2002, while I was doing research for *The Tex-Mex Cookbook*, I sat down with Martinez at the original Mariano's Mexican Cuisine restaurant in Dallas, which is no longer in existence. The bar menu offered lots of top-shelf tequilas, but I ordered one of Mariano's original frozen margaritas.

The tequila was really little more than a background flavor. The salt on the rim and the sweetness of the drink mix were far more pronounced than the liquor—which made the drink very popular with college kids and other imbibers on training wheels.

Over several of the icy cocktails, Martinez repeated the frozen margarita saga, a tale he has told countless times before: "When my father [Mariano Martinez Sr.] opened his restaurant, El Charro, in the 1950s, you couldn't sell liquor by the drink in Texas. But he made frozen margaritas for people who brought their own tequila."

Martinez's frozen margarita was an adaptation of the frozen daiquiri, which had been popularized by the unlikely trio of Ernest Hemingway, Fred Waring, and John F. Kennedy. In the 1930s, Hemingway waxed eloquent about the frozen daiquiris at La Floridita bar in Havana, where they were made using shaved ice. Musician Fred Waring launched the blender in the late 1930s and sold hundreds of thousands of them before World War Two by whipping up instant frozen daiquiris wherever he went. JFK drank frozen daiquiris before dinner in the White House, which gave the drink a burst of publicity in the 1960s.

The blender recipe for a frozen daiquiri was rum, lime juice, ice, and a sweetener. Substitute tequila for rum and you get a frozen margarita. The drink was little more than a curiosity in the 1960s, a way to use that souvenir bottle of tequila you brought home from your Mexican vacation.

"When I opened this restaurant in 1971, people came to me for margaritas, too," says Martinez. "Dad gave me his recipe—it was tequila, lime juice, and

FATHER OF the frozen margarita, Mariano Martinez (left), with Trini Lopez

orange liqueur. His secret ingredient was a splash of simple syrup. You put it in the blender with ice until it got slushy."

When cocktails became legal, Martinez wanted to make Mariano's Mexican Cuisine the Dallas destination for frozen margaritas. "I taught my bartender how to make the drink, but people complained about it. They said it tasted different every time. I tried to talk to the bartender about it one night, but he was sick of squeezing all those limes and threatened to quit," remembered Martinez.

"The next morning I was getting coffee at the Seven-Eleven and saw some kids getting icees out of the machine," he said. "That's when it hit me." 7-Eleven wasn't eager to help him purchase the machines, so Martinez ended up buying a soft-serve ice cream machine. "We tinkered with the machine and the recipe for a long time," he laughed. "We had a lot of tasting parties."

When you make a frozen margarita in a blender, you dilute the drink with added ice, he explained. But

if you put the same ingredients in an ice cream machine they won't freeze because the alcohol content is too high. First, he experimented with diluting the solution with enough water to allow it to freeze. But the resulting cocktail tasted too weak. The solution, Martinez told me, was to increase the sugar. With a high enough brix level (the scientific measurement of sugar content), you can freeze quite a bit of alcohol.

The sweet frozen margaritas at Mariano's Mexican Cuisine became an instant sensation. The Dallas Cowboys drank them; Trini Lopez and Lee Trevino drank them. But it was coeds from nearby Southern Methodist University who really spread the drink's fame. Mariano Martinez now owns several successful Tex-Mex restaurants in Dallas, and all of them serve margaritas.

Mariano Martinez never received a patent or trademark for his idea. He doesn't think it would have been possible anyway. "I just started making margaritas in a machine that already existed," he shrugged.

"I go places now and I tell people I invented the frozen margarita, and they say, 'Yeah, right.'"

fajitas more popular than old-fashioned combo platters.

"The frozen margarita made tequila an acceptable drink for women," observed Marc N. Scheinman, marketing professor at Pace University's Lubin School of Business and the author of a study titled "The Global Market for Tequila."

"The spread of the frozen margarita coincided with large numbers of young women coming into the workforce," said Scheinman. "It also coincided with a rise in immigration and the Mexicanization of American cuisine."

The frozen margarita rocked the liquor business. Between 1975 and 1995, tequila sales in the United States increased more than 1,500 percent. From 1995 to 2005, sales doubled again. In the early 1990s, tequila producers were overwhelmed by the demand. They were running out of agave. The potential loss of revenues prompted the regulatory body that supervises tequila production in Mexico to liberalize the rules.

Whereas all tequila was once made with 100 percent agave, now tequila could be distilled from 51 percent agave supplemented with cane sugar. The result was cheap tequila bottled solely for the

Mayo Bessan

Proprietor of

Cadillac Bar and Buffet

purpose of making margaritas. The cheap tequilas gave the frozen margarita a bad name and inspired tequila lovers to become more discerning in their purchases. Shaken margaritas, sometimes known as "Mexican martinis" were considered better showcases for premium tequilas.

The United States surpassed Mexico in tequila consumption in 2000 and the market continues to grow, fueled by the nation's insatiable demand for margaritas. In Mexico, where tequila is a macho drink taken neat with a chaser, the American frozen cocktail is beginning to make headway among Mexican women. The drink is also gaining ground in Europe and other parts of the world as Tex-Mex continues to grow in popularity.

In August 2005, Brown-Forman, the liquor marketing giant that owns Jack Daniel's, bought the Herradura tequila distillery for $876 million. At a time when all other categories of hard liquor were either declining or showing flat sales, liquor companies spent their money on the only category that showed any growth. The next time you fire up the blender, consider the way the frozen tequila cocktail redefined the way we eat.

EXPENSIVE TEQUILA

Reposado and *añejo* tequilas are aged in oak casks so they are easy to sip, and their mellow flavor is lost in a glass of lime juice. Making a frozen margarita with expensive tequila is like making a whiskey sour with single-malt scotch.

The bold, vegetal flavor of *plata* (silver) tequila makes a great margarita. Low-end 100-percent-agave tequilas start at around fifteen dollars a bottle and they are a good choice for frozen margaritas.

Super-premium tequilas, like Centinela, Herradura, El Tesoro, and Chinaco, go for between thirty and sixty dollars a bottle. Super-premium tequilas account for 7.4 percent of the 4.5 million cases of tequila that sold in the United States in 2006. And sales of super-premiums are growing at about 15 percent a year.

Beyond super-premium, there are the new ultra-premiums, which include Don Julio Real tequila at $312 and Gran Patrón Platinum at $203 a bottle. The most expensive tequila sold in Texas is Herradura Seleccion Suprema at $342 for a 750-milliliter bottle.

SMU Frozen Margarita

MAKES 1 LARGE OR 2 SMALL FROZEN MARGARITAS

WHAT'S THE FIRST THING YOU OFFER YOUR GUESTS WHEN THEY come over for dinner or a patio fiesta? A cold drink, of course. So let's start things off right. Personally, I like my margaritas frozen. If I am going to drink good tequila, I'd rather drink it straight up.

3 shots tequila plata
1 shot Grand Marnier
½ cup frozen limeade concentrate
2 cups crushed ice
Coarse salt
Lime wedge

Combine the tequila, Grand Marnier, limeade concentrate, and crushed ice in a blender and puree until slushy. Put the salt in a saucer. Wet the rim of a margarita glass with the lime wedge. Invert the glass in the saucer and coat the rim with salt. Pour the frozen drink into the salted glass.

VARIATIONS

PSYCHEDELIC PURPLE SWIRL MARGARITAS
Pour a shot of pomegranate concentrate into a salted glass, then pour the slush over the top so it swirls throughout.

ASTROTURF GREEN SWIRL MARGARITAS
Pour a shot of Midori melon liqueur into a salted glass, then pour the slush over the top so it swirls throughout.

WAITER WITH a tray
of hot plates in the
kitchen of the origi-
nal Cadillac Bar

Classic Shaken Margarita

MAKES 1

DRINK THIS ONE LIKE A MARTINI, STRAIGHT UP IN A CHILLED glass.

    2 shots Cuervo 1800 Reposado tequila
    ½ shot Cointreau
    ½ shot Grand Marnier
    1 shot freshly squeezed lime juice
    ½ shot Simple Syrup (recipe follows)
    3 shots sweet and sour mix (or limeade)

Shake all the ingredients in an ice-filled shaker for at least a minute and then strain into a margarita glass filled with ice. Garnish with a lime wheel.

Simple Syrup

MAKES ½ CUP

    1 cup sugar

In a pan over medium heat, combine the sugar with ½ cup of water. Stir until dissolved. Cool and store in a jar or bottle with a lid.

MARIACHIS AT La Margarita restaurant in San Antonio

FIVE COOL MARIACHI REQUESTS

The strolling musicians are really ripping it up. You've had a few margaritas and you're all caught up in the spirit. So when the mariachi band appears at your table, you hand them a couple of bucks and sit back to savor the serenade.

"What would you like to hear?" asks the guy with the big guitar. You open your mouth but nothing comes out. What are you going to request? They just played "La Bamba," "Guantanamera," and "Rancho Grande" for the clueless gringos at the last table.

Here's a list of five very cool mariachi songs:

1. "TÚ, SÓLO TÚ" (unrequited love)

Note the easy-to-remember title, which means "you only you." This Pedro Infante song makes quite an impression on first dates. "See how I'm going around, woman, drunken and passionate for your love..."

2. "VOLVER, VOLVER"
(broken-hearted about a girl)

This José Alfredo Jiménez classic is one of the best tears-in-the-beer songs ever written. All the drunk guys at the bar will join in on the chorus.

3. "MI RANCHITO"
(broken-hearted about a ranch)

Does he miss the little ranch or the woman he left behind there more? I'm guessing the ranch.

4. "PA' TODO EL AÑO"
(to kick off a suicidal year-long binge)

My personal favorite is about a guy planning to drink a whole year away and blame it on a woman. "I'm brave enough not to deny it, and I'll shout that it's for your love that I am killing myself."

5. "GRITENME PIEDRAS DEL CAMPO"
(talking to the landscape in love)

Extra credit for remembering the difficult title. Great for occasions when you're out of control and conversing with inanimate objects: "Talk to me, mountains and valleys. Scream to me, stones in the field. When have you ever seen anyone love like I am loving, cry like I am crying, die like I am dying."

Watermelon Margaritas

MAKES 4

THANKS TO GRAMERCY TAVERN MANAGER NICK MAUTONE FOR
the frozen watermelon ice cube idea.

½ small watermelon
8 ounces Simple Syrup (page 38)
4 ounces freshly squeezed lemon juice
4 ounces freshly squeezed lime juice
12 ounces gold tequila
8 ounces watermelon liqueur
12 mint leaves

Cut the watermelon into 1-inch cubes, removing the seeds as you go. Place
the cubes in a colander set inside a bowl. Stir the cubes gently to extract juice
without breaking up the cubes. You should have at least 8 ounces of juice. Put
the watermelon cubes on a tray and freeze until solid—about an hour.

Mix the syrup, lemon juice, and lime juice with the watermelon juice.
To serve, divide the frozen cubes among 4 glasses. Add the tequila, then the
liqueur, and then the juice mixture and stir. Garnish with the mint leaves.

THE LATE Matt Martinez
Jr. with a frozen marga-
rita outside his family's
restaurant in Austin

THE MENU at the original Cadillac Bar featured steaks, chops, wild game, spaghetti and meatballs, and New Orleans shrimp Creole along with baked *cabrito* and a Mexican dinner

Ramos Gin Fizz

MAKES 1

FIZZES AND FLIPS ARE MAKING A COMEBACK AMONG "CRAFT
cocktail" enthusiasts. If no liquor stores or supermarkets in your area sell
powdered egg whites or orange flower water, look for these ingredients at baking supply stores or online.

1½ ounces dry gin
½ ounce freshly squeezed lemon juice
½ ounce freshly squeezed lime juice
2 tablespoons cream
1 egg white (or powdered egg whites)
¼ ounce club soda, plus more to taste
1 tablespoon powdered sugar
3 to 4 dashes of orange flower water (essential, but hard to find)

Combine all ingredients except the extra club soda in a cocktail shaker with a
scoop of ice and shake until the mixture foams. Strain into a wine glass and top
off with club soda.

CADILLAC "EGG DRINKS"

THERE WERE more than half a dozen "egg drinks" on the menu at the Cadillac Bar, including four fizzes and
three flips. Egg drinks became rare because of the labor involved to make them and because of a fear of
salmonella contamination from raw eggs. The drink has to be shaken for quite a while to get the ice cubes to
agitate the eggs enough to cause them to foam. In New Orleans, the drink was shaken for up to five minutes;
sometimes the shaker was passed from one bartender to another. You can cheat and whip the drink without
ice in your blender. Powdered egg whites take the fear out of using eggs.

TEXAS RED GRAPEFRUIT

The first red grapefruit was discovered in Texas in 1929 growing on a pink grapefruit tree. Horticulturists at Texas A&M University developed the Ruby Red cultivar from the seeds of that natural mutation. While changing citrus groves from one variety to another is usually a long process, severe freezes in the 1950s speeded up the replanting process in South Texas. As a result, Texas quickly acquired the reputation as the leading producer of red grapefruit.

In an attempt to stimulate more mutations, scientists bombarded red grapefruit seeds and budshoots with gamma rays. That's how the Rio Red variety was developed. And when two more severe freezes in the 1980s killed many older trees, much of the valley was replanted in this new redder variety. Those trees are now bearing the new generation of grapefruit. While the deep ruby color probably doesn't make the Rio Red grapefruit taste any better, thanks to high levels of lycopene, it might make it better for your health. Both pink and red grapefruits contain lycopene, but the highest

concentrations are in the reddest grapefruit, such as the Rio Star.

The names of the varieties get pretty confusing. Marketing executives are trying to sell "Texas red grapefruit" as a blanket term. But there is a difference between the cultivars. Rio Star and Ruby Red are the two varieties you are most likely to see. They both taste about the same, but the new Rio Star variety is darker red and keeps its color throughout the season. Ruby Red is the original red grapefruit. Its color fades to pink as the season progresses. While other states grow these varieties too, Texas-grown red grapefruit regularly trounces all competitors in blind tastings.

The secret of the great taste is something growers call the "sugar to acid ratio." While Texas grapefruits actually have about the same sugar level as comparable fruit from other places, they have less acid and therefore less sourness. Texas growers brag that they have "taken the pucker out of grapefruit."

Salty Perro Rojo

MAKES 1

WITH ITS ROSY COLOR AND SWEET FLAVOR, TEXAS RED GRAPE-
fruit juice makes an outstanding cocktail. Grapefruit juice and gin is known as
a Greyhound, and if you salt the rim of the glass, it's a Salty Dog. If you substitute tequila for the gin, it's a Salty Perro. Since the grapefruit juice is red, I call
this drink a Salty Perro Rojo. Columnist Gustavo Arellano taste-tested a few
of these at my house one day and gave this cocktail the "¡Ask A Mexican!" seal
of approval.

> Coarse sea salt
> 4 shots freshly squeezed red grapefruit juice
> 1 shot plata tequila

Put the salt in a saucer and wet the rim of a highball glass with grapefruit juice.
Salt the glass by dipping the wet rim in the salt. Fill the salted glass with ice. Add
the tequila, then the juice, and stir carefully so as not to mess up the salted rim.

Michelada

MAKES 1

MICHELADA MEANS "MY COLD BEER" IN SPANISH. IT'S A COLD
beer, alright—with some extra seasonings thrown in the mug. Here's a standard
recipe. If you're serving from a Bloody Mary bar, your guests can doctor the beer
themselves.

> ½ lime
> Coarse sea salt
> 2 dashes Worcestershire sauce
> 1 teaspoon Tabasco or other hot pepper sauce
> 12 ounces Mexican beer

Salt the rim of a chilled beer mug by rubbing it with the lime and dipping it in
the coarse salt. Squeeze the lime into the mug. Add the Worcestershire and
Tabasco. Pour in the beer and serve.

MEXICAN BEER

A wave of German and Czech (Bohemian and Moravian) immigration in the mid to late 1800s supplied Mexico with skilled brewers and influenced its style of beer-making forever after. Founded in 1890, Monterrey's Cervecería Cuauhtémoc Moctezuma was the first major brewery in Mexico. Brands that are popular in the United States include Dos Equis (XX) Amber, a lighter style of a Viennese lager, and Bohemia, which is modeled after a Czech pilsner.

Negra Modelo, a dark and malty Vienna lager, is produced by Cervecería Cuauhtémoc's competitor, Grupo Modelo, in Mexico City. The second largest brewery in the country, Grupo Modelo also makes the number-one-selling Mexican beer in the United States, Corona.

In 1998 a microbrewery began producing remarkable small-batch ales under the name Casta (Spanish for "purity") in Monterrey. Casta Dorada ("golden") is a slightly sweet brew with cinnamon aromas. Casta Bruna is an excellent English-style brown ale, while Casta Morena ("brunette") is a thick and creamy stout. Many beer geeks think Casta makes the best beers Mexico has to offer.

It's nearly impossible to find in the United States, so if you're looking for a souvenir to bring home from Monterrey, consider bringing home a case of Castas.

MY TOP 10 TEXAS MICROBREWERY BEERS

The first breweries in Texas appeared around 1840 in areas settled by Germans. These tiny operations would be called craft breweries today: they made highly individual beers in small quantities for local markets. Without ice or refrigeration, they could only brew during the colder months.

In 1877 the king of German lager-style breweries, Anheuser-Busch of St. Louis, came to Texas. There were some seventy breweries in the state when Anheuser-Busch arrived. The national brewery sold a consistent lager beer, advertised heavily, and bought up Texas ice houses. Undercapitalized and unable to compete, native Texas breweries began to decline. By the time Prohibition arrived in 1918, there were only eighteen breweries left in Texas.

Texas microbreweries are now making a comeback. Some of the beers brewed in small Texas operations have won national acclaim. Here's a list of my favorite modern Texas microbrews:

AVAILABLE YEAR-ROUND:

1. SAINT ARNOLD ELISSA
If you love crisp, bitter, hoppy beers, you will fall hard for this India Pale Ale (IPA) named after Galveston's tall ship.

2. LIVE OAK PILZ
Live Oak beers are sold on draft to select pubs and restaurants around the state that cater to beer lovers. All of their beers are extremely well made, but the Czech-style pilsner is spectacular.

3. REAL ALE FULL MOON PALE RYE ALE
The hippest brewer in Texas, Real Ale in Blanco makes this unusually crisp, rye-flavored ale that goes exceptionally well with food.

4. RAHR & SONS UGLY PUG
The Fort Worth microbrewery's number-one seller is a German *schwartzbier* made with dark roasted malts for a rich flavor and dark color.

5. SHINER BOHEMIAN BLACK LAGER
Another German *schwartzbier;* this one was made to celebrate the brewery's anniversary, but it was so popular it's now made year round. Shiner's number-two seller after Shiner Bock and much more interesting.

SEASONAL FAVORITES:

6. REAL ALE SHADE GROWN COFFEE PORTER
Available on draught in the wintertime, this intense porter is made with Katz fair-trade coffee.

7. SAINT ARNOLD SUMMER PILS
Crisp, refreshing, delicious summer Czech-style pilsner.

8. RAHR & SONS BUCKING BOCK
A sweet, golden Maibock (spring bock) that's shockingly good.

9. LIVE OAK HEFEWEIZEN
You can get this spring and summer wheat beer with live yeast and citrus flavors on draught only—but it's one of the best HefeWeizens in the country.

10. SAINT ARNOLD CHRISTMAS ALE
Lots of malt, lots of hops, and lots of alcohol make this sweet, spicy, hearty ale a favorite for the holiday season.

SAN ANTONIO Brewer's Association members, 1895

DO-IT-YOURSELF Bloody
Mary buffet at the Cadillac
Bar in Houston

Cadillac's Bloody Mary Bar

MAKES 5 CUPS

AT THE CADILLAC BAR IN HOUSTON, THEY SET UP A "BLOODY Mary Bar" during weekend brunch. Patrons doctor up their own Bloody Marys with the sauces and condiments of their choice. A Bloody Mary bar is a great idea at home for a brunch or football watching party. You can offer a choice of vodka or tequila (for Bloody Marias) and cold beer for Michelada fans, and your guests can make their drinks the way they like them. Nobody can blame you for making their drinks too weak or too strong, either.

BLOODY MARY MIX

1 quart Spicy V-8
3 tablespoons Worcestershire sauce
Juice of a Mexican or Key lime
1 tablespoon red pepper flakes
1 tablespoon cracked black pepper
1 teaspoon minced fresh cilantro

FOR THE BAR

Vodka
Tequila
Celery stalks
Olives
Cocktail onions
Celery salt
Prepared horseradish
Worcestershire sauce
Tabasco and other bottled hot sauces
Black pepper
Sea salt

Combine all mix ingredients, stir well, and place in the refrigerator until well chilled. To make the Bloody Mary Bar, pour the mix into a pitcher and put it on the bar along with bottles of vodka and tequila, ice, and celery stalks and other condiments and invite your guests to make their own Bloody Marys.

The mix will last for up to 2 days, covered and refrigerated.

FRESHLY GRILLED
fajitas, Ninfa's on
Navigation in Houston

\#3

DISAPPEARING SKIRTS AND THE NEW FAJITAS

CAREFUL, HOT PLATE!" THE WAITER SAID. THE DARK brown fajitas at Houston's Original Ninfa's on Navigation came on a sizzling cast-iron comal with lots of caramelized onions. The beef was cooked well-done and cut into thin strips against the coarse grain. It was so tough you had to pinch the tortilla to keep from pulling the meat strips out with your teeth when you took a bite. But the beef was very flavorful.

"It's Certified Hereford outside skirt steak. It's not marinated at all, it's just seasoned with salt and pepper and brushed lightly with soy sauce as it comes off the grill," according to the Ninfa's meat buyer, an outspoken chef named Mark Mavrantonis.

Faja means "belt," and *fajita* means "little belt," a reference to the shape of the diaphragm muscle known as the outside skirt. Ninfa's has to pay "a pretty penny" to get the hard-to-come-by USDA Choice outside skirt steaks, Mavrantonis said. Ninfa's restaurants are the only places in Texas where I have seen American outside skirt in the last few years, and they serve it there to preserve an old tradition.

The Original Ninfa's on Navigation is the restaurant that made fajitas famous. Thank goodness they still taste like they did in the old days. According to a company press release that came out in 2002, "It is a fact that a true legend of the food business, Mama Ninfa Laurenzo of Houston, Texas, originated the first fajita in the United States in 1973."

This is one of many claims that have been made about the invention of fajitas. Success has a thousand fathers, as they say—and this success has at least one Mama.

Mama Ninfa was born Maria Ninfa Rodriguez in 1924 in the Lower Rio Grande Valley. She married Domenic Thomas Laurenzo, an Italian American from Rhode Island. In 1949, the couple opened the Rio Grande Tortilla Company on Navigation Boulevard in Houston. Twenty years later, Laurenzo died. In 1973, Mama Ninfa opened a restaurant in the front room of the tortilla factory with ten tables and forty chairs. On her first day, she sold 250 *tacos al carbon*. The meat was skirt steak, a cut she knew well.

"I grew up in the Lower Rio Grande Valley," Mama Ninfa told me on the phone in 2003, a year before she died. "When I opened the restaurant, I was just serving the same kind of good honest food that we used to eat at home. Fajitas were an old family recipe." Mama Ninfa never claimed she had invented fajitas; she just brought the tradition of grilling secondary cuts of beef on a mesquite grill and serving the meat chopped up with condiments and flour tortillas from the Lower Rio Grande Valley to Houston.

A much bolder claim was made by Juan Antonio "Sonny" Falcon, the man who calls himself the Fajita King. Some years ago, under a tent set up on Auditorium Shores for the Hill Country Wine

THE LATE Mama Ninfa at Ninfa's on Navigation

and Food Festival in Austin, I served on a Tex-Mex panel discussion with Falcon. Sonny grew up in Mercedes, Texas, and worked there for a while as a butcher. During the 1960s, while working at the meat counter of Guajardo's Cash Grocery in East Austin, Falcon claims he gave "fajitas" their name while he experimented with the diaphragm muscle. "It looked like a little belt," he said. Falcon can document the first time he sold fajitas to the public. It was at a Diez y Seis celebration in Kyle in September 1969.

Falcon's fame drew a big crowd to our tent at the food festival, including a couple of hecklers. His fellow Tejanos from the Lower Rio Grande Valley loudly contended that their grandmothers were making fajitas before Falcon was born.

"I like Sonny Falcon, I went to school with him. But he didn't invent fajitas," said Liborio "Libo" Hinojosa whose family owns H&H Meat Products in Mercedes, one of the Valley's biggest meat suppliers, "The Lion Mart in Brownsville was selling fajitas at their meat counter way before 1969."

I N THE LOWER RIO GRANDE VALLEY, the restaurant most often credited with the invention of fajitas is the Round-Up, in Pharr, which is no longer in business. There the dish was called *botanas*. The owner, Tila Garza, put grilled skirt steak on top of a plate of nachos and chalupas with some guacamole and lettuce around it and served it as a free botanas, or happy-hour snack. It was so popular she started selling the platter instead of giving it away. And then she put the fajita meat on a sizzling comal and added it to the menu.

"When I got back from Vietnam in the early 1970s, the Round-Up was wildly popular," remembered Joe Alonso, who once owned several Tex-Mex restaurants in the Lower Rio Grande Valley. "I had a restaurant called Senorial in Alamo at the time," Alonso said. "Everybody came in and asked for a botanas platter." Alonso recalled that Senorial was the second restaurant to serve the fajitas-covered botanas. But instead of serving a communal platter, Alonso served his fajitas botanas on individual plates with rice and beans on the side.

Outside skirt went from a dollar a pound in 1971 to $4.79 a pound in 2008. Dr. Gary Smith, a professor in the Texas A&M animal sciences department, encouraged a graduate student named Homero Recio to take a trip to South Texas to trace the origins of fajitas. In his paper on the subject, Recio stated that the term had been in use among butchers of the Lower Rio Grande Valley since the 1940s. According to Recio, the actual originators of what we call fajita tacos were the Hispanic ranch hands who were given the head, intestines, and other unwanted beef cuts such as the diaphragm as part of their pay. They pounded the diaphragm, marinated it with lime juice, and grilled it, then cut it up and ate the meat with salsa and condiments on flour tortillas. Although the name *fajita* and the serving style is unique to Texas, a similar grilled diaphragm "steak" is also common in Nuevo León, where it is called *arrachera al carbón*.

The first restaurant to popularize fajitas in Austin in the early 1970s was the Hyatt Regency hotel. The beef was served on a sizzling comal with onions and peppers and the signature spread of tortillas, guacamole, salsa, and condiments. But the hotel chef at the Hyatt balked at serving chewy skirt steak. Instead, he substituted sirloin. It wasn't long afterward that chicken fajitas made their debut. The fact that chickens don't have skirt steaks didn't seem to bother anyone.

F AJITAS ARE THE HEART OF MODERN Tex-Mex. They became popular because consumers were rejecting Americanized combination plates in the 1970s and 1980s in favor of more authentic Mexican cuisine. Fajitas weren't actually Mexican, of course, but at least they represented authentic Tejano cuisine. Texas-Mexicans didn't eat cheese enchiladas in chili gravy at home—but they did eat fajitas.

Fajitas revived Tex-Mex at a crucial point in its history and went on to become its signature dish. Obviously, a cookbook called *The Tex-Mex Grill* needs to features some fajita recipes.

But outside skirt steak, the cut that makes the best fajitas, has all but disappeared from retail meat markets. Every supermarket and butcher shop I vis-

ited said no one sold them anymore. I tried the inside skirts, which are still widely available—and they were so tough, my table mates declared them inedible.

And then there were the insane prices. Angus inside skirt was selling for the same price as USDA Prime steaks. Why cook tough fajita meat when prime steak was cheaper? To get a handle on the current state of beef I called the agricultural extension service.

At Papa Perez Mexican restaurant in downtown Bryan I split a one-pound order of grilled fajitas with two meat scientists from the Department of Animal Science at Texas A&M University, Meat Science Section leader Dr. Jeff Savell and professor Dr. Davey Griffin. The fajita beef was tender and nicely browned and was served with grilled onions on a sizzling comal. As we made our tacos, I asked them about beef prices.

The demand for expensive steaks was flagging, so prices were falling, I was told. Meanwhile fajitas were in short supply. In 1988, the U.S.-Japan Beef and Citrus Agreement reclassified outside skirt,

the cut that started the fajita craze, as tariff-free offal. The Japanese, who used to pay the equivalent of a 200 percent tariff on U.S. beef, can now buy our outside skirt steak with no tariff at all. They are currently importing 90 percent of it.

Meat companies have compensated by offering some new cuts to restaurants. In fact, the Texas A&M meat scientists were working on new cuts used for fajitas and bistro steaks. The meat doctors started rhapsodizing about wedges, flaps, hangers, and tails. At the time, it sounded like they were discussing airplane parts.

"What kind of meat do you use in your fajitas?" I asked the restaurant manager at Papa Perez when he stopped by our table.

"We use inside skirt steak," he said. "It's already marinated when we buy it. Then we add our own seasonings."

"It sure doesn't get this tender when I grill it," I said, poking at the taco meat on my plate.

Then the meat experts let me in on the secret: enzymes. To create tender beef fajitas like the ones on our sizzling comal, meat processors treat tough inner skirt with chemical enzymes or natural enzymes such as papain, which is extracted from papaya.

Papain is tricky. It doesn't start softening up the meat until it is activated by a temperature of around 122°F. And once it starts, it doesn't stop until the meat cools. If you have ever had fajitas that tasted like mush, it's because the restaurant cooked them too slow or kept papain-treated meat in the warmer or on the steam table too long after it was cooked.

You can get papain in the grocery store; it's the active ingredient in Adolph's meat tenderizer. All I had to do was come up with some marinade recipes with papain and backyard barbecuers could make tender inside skirt steak at home, right?

No, it wasn't quite that simple, the scientists said. When you marinate meat at home, you are lucky to get a 2 percent "take-up rate," as the measure of absorption is known in the biz. To increase the take-up rate, commercial meat packers do their marinating in a commercial vacuum tumbler. Mechanically tumbling the meat and the marinade in a rotating vacuum container with paddles breaks up and stretches out the protein fibers, increasing the meat's ability to absorb the liquid.

With as little as twenty minutes of vacuum tumbling, the "take-up" ratio can be increased to 10 percent. Along with the tenderizer and spices, salt and phosphate are also added to increase moisture retention. That makes the meat juicier and pads the meat packers' profits by increasing the weight.

But it gets even more complicated. There isn't enough inside skirt steak to satisfy the demand for fajitas, which is why the meat scientists are experimenting with other cuts. These mechanically

SIZZLING FAJITAS AT LA MARGARITA

The twenty-four-hour Tex-Mex restaurant and bakery known as Mi Tierra is an institution in San Antonio. The restaurant got its start when Pete Cortez took over a taco stand in the Mercado in the 1930s. The restaurant expanded several times, taking over most of the adjacent spaces. In 1981, Cortez bought the Produce Row Oyster Bar a few doors down the street and gave it to his son, Jorge, who renamed it La Margarita. Jorge decided to feature fajitas and frozen margaritas at the new restaurant, though they weren't very popular in San Antonio at the time. He remembers his father's reaction.

"He said we should work on the menu together, and I told him the menu was already printed," chuckles Jorge. "He was shocked. Then I showed it to him. The menu had fajitas by the pound. He got really angry. The worst part was, I couldn't even open the place to prove it would work because I was waiting for these comals and wooden holders I had ordered in Monterrey. Nobody was doing the sizzling fajitas thing in San Antonio yet. I saw meat served that way in Monterrey and I loved the idea, so I ordered a lot of comals down there. But it took a long time to get them. My dad almost killed me. One of the greatest days of my life came a few years later when the restaurant was doing really well and my dad said, 'Son, that was a pretty good idea.'"

La Margarita has become famous for its frozen margaritas, sizzling fajitas, and strolling mariachis. The restaurant still sells Texas oysters on the half shell, too.

tumbled, enzyme-treated meat cuts are all sold interchangeably under the umbrella term "beef for fajitas." You can sample this faux fajita meat at any taqueria in Texas.

Marketing mystery meats under generic names like "beef for fajitas" runs counter to everything being preached in the food world. It's exactly the kind of deceptive marketing Eric Schlosser and Michael Pollan have pointed out in their books.

Inspired by *The Omnivore's Dilemma*, in which Michael Pollan goes hunting and butchers a wild hog, young urban food lovers are seeking to understand and deepen their own relationships with meat.

The local food movement has impressed consumers with the importance of provenance. Customers at farmer's markets are contracting for whole lambs and pigs and people are forming co-ops to share sides of grass-fed beef. Urbanites nationwide are signing up for butchery classes. Food lovers are interested in learning how to cook the whole animal. They are ordering organ meat at restaurants, looking for short ribs and soup bones at the grocery store, and trying to cure their own bacon at home.

But the "get to know your meat" movement looks a little different from Texas. And Pollan's sense of irony about an intellectual like himself wielding a rifle sounds pretty silly if you hunt routinely. Yet, like meat eaters across the country, I wanted to know where my meat was coming from.

The Texas A&M meat scientists suggested that if I wanted to understand the new fajitas and what's happening in the fast-changing field of meat fabrication, I needed to learn a little bit about butchery myself. So when we got back to their office, they handed me an application for a class called Beef 101.

THE FRONT END OF A BEEF CARCASS was dangling from the ceiling. With a butcher's hook and a boning knife in my hands, I regarded the bright-red expanse of raw meat. The day before, I had patted this steer on the forehead. On the first day of Beef 101 class, we met at the Texas A&M Beef Center in the rural farmland outside College Station.

THE BEEF 101 class estimated the yield and grade of steers on the hoof

As far as butchery classes go, the three-day class called Beef 101 at Texas A&M is the granddaddy of them all and way ahead of the trend. Davey Griffin set up the first class more than twenty years ago. It's a comprehensive overview of the beef industry from stockyard to cutting floor offered three times a year, and it's almost always booked solid with food-industry pros.

After several hours of classroom work, we adjourned to the barn out back, where we estimated the grades of six cattle on the hoof, guessing at yield and quality by petting, stroking, and poking the apprehensive animals—just like cattle buyers at an auction barn. We nicknamed the fattest one Porky and predicted a Choice grade (it turned out that we were right).

There isn't much money in cattle raising. Other than a few giants like the King Ranch, most Texas cattle ranchers are little guys. One of the students in the class works for ConocoPhillips in Houston and has a weekend place near Bryan, where he raises cattle to "get the kids away from the TV." Half of the cattle in Texas are raised on ranches with fewer than fifty head by retirees, hobbyists, and plain folks trying to avoid property taxes with an agricultural exemption.

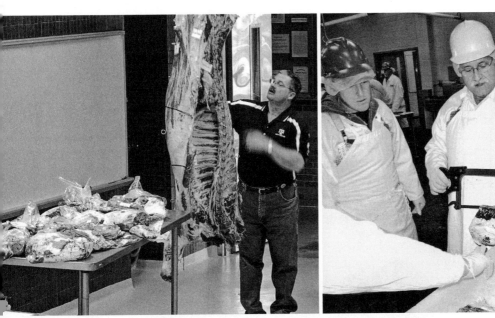

PROFESSOR DAVEY Griffin (left) giving an anatomy lesson with a side of beef. Professor Jeff Savell (right) demonstrating the use of a meat saw.

My other classmates included a couple butchers from a country grocery store, a guy who wants to open a small meat plant, several chefs, and a lot of food-industry marketing people. We followed the cattle truck over to the Rosenthal Meat Science and Technology Center on campus, a working meat-processing plant. While we watched, a medium-size Angus cross we'll call Blacky walked down the chute and through the sliding metal door to a small enclosure that he barely fit into. Meat Center manager Ray Riley demonstrated the "cash knocker."

Riley loaded what looked like a .22 blank into the long-handled device and centered the mushroom-shaped business end of it on Blacky's forehead. Then he pulled a trigger in the handle, and after a loud report, the animal fell to the ground unconscious. A trap door and tilting floor opened and the device rolled Blacky over to three waiting students who fixed one of his rear legs to a chain that hung from a motor in the ceiling.

The motor pulled the chain and the body up so it dangled overhead. A student with a knife made a foot-long slash between the brisket and throat, and Blacky started bleeding profusely. It takes six to eight minutes to bleed out, and it's important that the animal remain alive so the heart can pump out all the blood. The animal dies after it bleeds out.

The feet were cut off and the still-twitching carcass moved along an overhead conveyor line called the "rail" while still hanging from the chain. At the next station, the hide was removed with a mechanical hide-puller, then came the evisceration, which was done by hand. The guts were sealed at each end to prevent spillage, and after an incision, the entrails were collected into a wheeled bucket to be sorted later. The head and tail were removed and cleaned.

Finally, the carcass was carefully inspected for bruises, hair, and fecal matter, and any contaminated areas were trimmed away. The whole carcass was cut in half, sprayed with lactic acid in an enclosed booth to retard microbial growth, and moved into the cooler. Blacky had ceased being Blacky and become a piece of beef.

Nobody got sick or left the class, but a lot of Beef 101 students were obviously grossed out. We all watched the process with the hushed reverence of a funeral, and we left with a new respect for both

ANGUS BEEF CHART

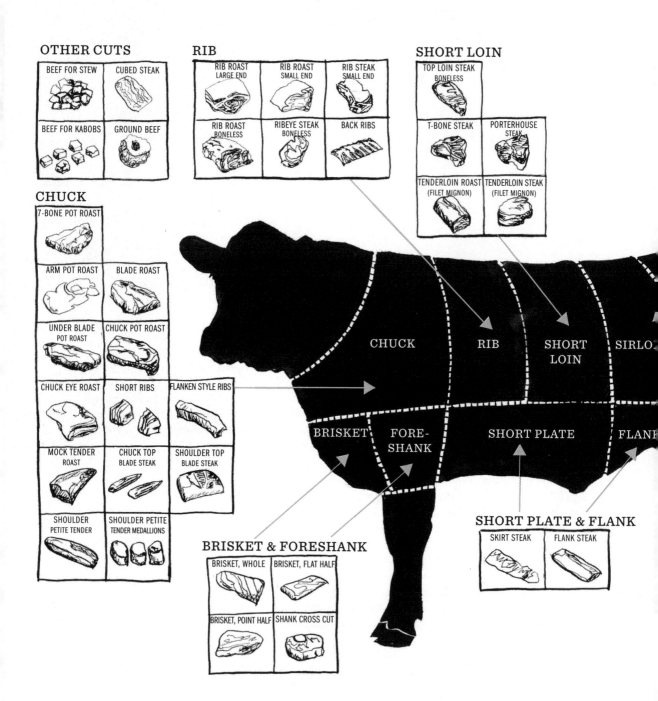

OTHER CUTS

BEEF FOR STEW	CUBED STEAK
BEEF FOR KABOBS	GROUND BEEF

RIB

RIB ROAST LARGE END	RIB ROAST SMALL END	RIB STEAK SMALL END
RIB ROAST BONELESS	RIBEYE STEAK BONELESS	BACK RIBS

SHORT LOIN

TOP LOIN STEAK BONELESS	
T-BONE STEAK	PORTERHOUSE STEAK
TENDERLOIN ROAST (FILET MIGNON)	TENDERLOIN STEAK (FILET MIGNON)

CHUCK

7-BONE POT ROAST		
ARM POT ROAST	BLADE ROAST	
UNDER BLADE POT ROAST	CHUCK POT ROAST	
CHUCK EYE ROAST	SHORT RIBS	FLANKEN STYLE RIBS
MOCK TENDER ROAST	CHUCK TOP BLADE STEAK	SHOULDER TOP BLADE STEAK
SHOULDER PETITE TENDER	SHOULDER PETITE TENDER MEDALLIONS	

CHUCK · RIB · SHORT LOIN · SIRLO

BRISKET · FORE-SHANK · SHORT PLATE · FLANK

BRISKET & FORESHANK

BRISKET, WHOLE	BRISKET, FLAT HALF
BRISKET, POINT HALF	SHANK CROSS CUT

SHORT PLATE & FLANK

SKIRT STEAK	FLANK STEAK

the people who work in slaughterhouses and the animals themselves.

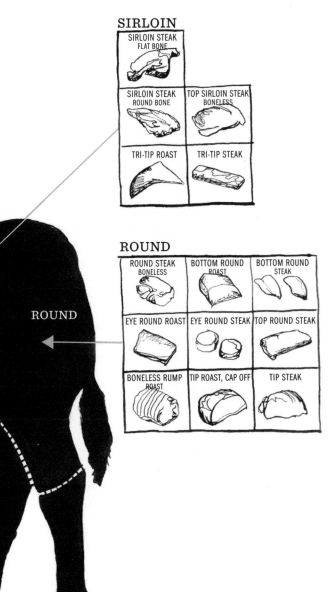

SIRLOIN

SIRLOIN STEAK FLAT BONE

SIRLOIN STEAK ROUND BONE

TOP SIRLOIN STEAK BONELESS

TRI-TIP ROAST

TRI-TIP STEAK

ROUND

ROUND STEAK BONELESS

BOTTOM ROUND ROAST

BOTTOM ROUND STEAK

EYE ROUND ROAST

EYE ROUND STEAK

TOP ROUND STEAK

BONELESS RUMP ROAST

TIP ROAST, CAP OFF

TIP STEAK

ROUND

DAY TWO OF BEEF 101 STARTED WITH an anatomy class by Griffin in which we learned the location of each cut of meat on a cattle skeleton nicknamed Bossy. There were some surprises. "This is the Infraspinatus muscle," said Griffin, holding up a plastic-wrapped cut of meat. "It is the second-tenderest cut of beef after the tenderloin—and it comes from the shoulder clod." Sometimes called the top blade, it is the cut that yields newly popular flatiron steaks.

After the lecture, we suited up. Dressed in a hair net and a hard hat, white frock and apron, a Kevlar glove and sleeve, and a metal chest protector, I strapped on my knife holder and entered the work area.

Led by Jeff Savell, my Beef 101 team took a meat saw to the four-hundred-pound side of beef, cutting it into chuck, rib, loin, and round—the four primals. The shoulder, or chuck, is the front end; that's where the brisket and shoulder clod come from. Most of it ends up as ground meat. The rib and loin yield the valuable "middle meats" prized in steak houses. The rump end is known as the round; it was once cut into giant round steaks, and now it yields such prizes as the eye of round roast.

To get the shoulder clod away in one piece, you gently sever the connective tissue that binds the meat to the shoulder blade while you pull down on the meat with the hook. Sliding the boning knife between the bone and the muscle without puncturing the meat requires a delicate touch, while yanking on the hook hard enough to pull the clod away demands brute force. It's an odd combination of skills—like playing the piano while moving it.

"Put your weight into it," the young A&M meat science major who served as my mentor encouraged. "I'll make sure it doesn't fall on the floor." I hung on the hook, and finally, the clod pulled away. We flopped it onto the worktable as if it were a thirty-pound fish.

Now we began to "fabricate" our final cuts. There are a lot of different ways to butcher a carcass. You can remove the whole tenderloin—or you can include it in porterhouse and T-bone steaks. You

THE NEW BISTRO STEAKS AND FAJITAS

Here are some of the newly popular cuts of beef you might find in the grocery-store meat case. We grill them and eat them fajita-style in Texas, but they are known as "bistro steaks" on the east and west coasts because of their popularity in the French bistro dish steak frites.

SIRLOIN FLAP, FLAP MEAT, FLAP STEAK
Called *bavette d'aloyau* in France, this is an abdominal muscle connected to the inside skirt. Butterflied very thin, it is a chewy but flavorful cut.

FLATIRON STEAK, TOP BLADE STEAK, TEXAS SIZZLER
The second most tender piece of meat on the steer after the tenderloin, this cut comes from the shoulder blade. The cut is shaped like a fish with a spine of tough connective tissue down the center. In Texas the "fish" is often cut into steaks called Texas sizzlers. When you fillet the "fish," you get two pieces that can be cut into flatiron steaks.

HANGER, HANGING TENDER
A wonderfully flavorful piece of meat that comes away when the animal is eviscerated. Like the outside skirt, the hanging tender was classified as offal under the Japanese tariff agreements; hence the Japanese buy almost all of it before we get any.

CHUCK STEAK, CHUCK TENDERS
Another relatively tender cut from the shoulder clod that's a bargain in Mexican meat markets.

TRI-TIP STEAK
A triangular piece from the sirloin that's tough, but makes great fajitas. Tri-tip roasts are the most popular barbecue meat in California.

BONELESS SHORT RIB
Known in Korean barbecue as *kalbi*, this highly marbled meat is excellent cut into thin sheets, flattened, marinated, and grilled.

can make rib-eye steaks with the bone in or without. Once upon a time, grocery-store butchers cut the shoulder blade into "seven-bone" pot roasts. Today, the same section of chuck yields flatiron steaks and shoulder tenders, cuts that are turning up in fancy restaurants as "bistro steaks." After we cut the fajita meat away from the ribs, we removed the first layer of the abdominal wall that's attached to it. That's the inside skirt, Savell told me.

After I learned how to cut up a shoulder clod to make flatiron steaks and tenders, I took a break and walked around. Griffin called me over and showed me a piece of boneless short rib so marbled the meat was as much white as red.

Savell pointed out the diaphragm muscle, the famous outside skirt steak. Since the meat runs in a circle around the inside of the thoracic cavity, it was easy to see where it got the "belt" name.

I got the tedious task of cleaning them both. There is a tough membrane to peel away and under that, there's a layer of silverskin connective tissue that has to be cut off with a knife.

There are two layers of abdominal muscle under the outside skirt. Some people called these tough cuts flap and tail meat, but since both used to go on the ground beef pile, nobody worried much about nomenclature. And that's how these pieces got lumped together as "beef for fajitas."

The more I thought about it, the more I realized that the word *fajitas* didn't mean anything.

O N MEMORIAL DAY WEEKEND, I grilled up fajitas for a family gathering. But before I let everyone dig in, I made them taste test four different kinds of "fajitas." The marinated sirloin flap was pretty popular; it beat out the marinated and unmarinated inside skirt and the marinated "beef for fajitas." The meat came from my brother Dave, who works for restaurant purveyor Ben E. Keith in San Antonio. At my request, he called in fajita samples from meat suppliers. Our taste test represented the most popular meats sold for fajitas in Texas restaurants.

The best restaurant meats we tried were marinated. We can thank vacuum tumbler technology for turning previously tough cuts into excellent

BONELESS SHORT rib is the most marbled cut of beef

fajitas. But as always, there's a catch. As one A&M meat scientist explained, the process of marinating beef faces the same inherent problem as grinding beef. If you start off with one spot of bacterial contamination on the surface of the meat, you end up spreading it very effectively throughout the entire batch. It's only a matter of time before we face the first marinated beef recall.

It helps that fajitas are usually cooked well-done. And adding antimicrobial agents to the marinade helps. But read the ingredient list and you have to conclude that you are eating beef in a complex chemical stew.

In another backyard barbecue, I cooked up four more varieties of fajita meat, this time based on what's available in retail meat markets. I bought marinated inside skirt and ribbon-cut short ribs,

and unmarinated chuck steak at a Mexican meat market. The skirt was the most expensive at $4.45 a pound. The other cuts were around $4. The store also sold *"res para fajitas,"* a hodgepodge of marinated beef trimmings for $2.98 a pound.

When I saw highly marbled boneless short-rib meat for $3.98 a pound at Costco, I impulsively picked some up. It was the same marbled meat that Dr. Griffin had shown me while we were cutting up our sides of beef in class. According to every recipe I could find, the short-rib meat contains lots of connective tissue and needs to be boiled before you put it on a barbecue. But I eat this stuff in Korean barbecue joints all the time—thin-sliced and raw.

I tried to butterfly the meat, but finally I gave up and put it on my handy Krups home meat slicer and cut it into slices about a fifth of an inch thick.

I pounded the meat very thin and seasoned it with my usual chile and garlic rub with some Adolph's meat tenderizer added.

The chuck steak won the taste test. The meat-market marinated inside skirt came in second. The ribbon-cut short ribs were good, but they didn't look like fajitas. The boneless short-rib meat was so tender it fell apart. In subsequent experiments I cut boneless short rib a little thicker and forgot the Adolph's. Marinated in a pineapple juice and soy sauce mixture, it was my favorite new fajita stand-in. Further experiments included tender flatiron steaks that I cut from chuck blade roasts and butter-flied tri-tip. The flatiron steak fajitas were outstanding. Cutting up the tri-tip was a bit of challenge.

JOE T. GARCIA'S IN FORT WORTH seats up to 1,500 people when all the patios are open. Fajitas are by far the most popular order; the tender beef served there takes no effort at all to chew, but it doesn't have a lot of flavorful char or coarse-grained character, either.

"We use tenderloin for our fajitas," Joe T.'s owner, Jody Lancarte, said. I was shocked.

Christine Lopez Martinez, the manager of Matt's Rancho Martinez in Dallas, another restaurant with great fajitas, said Matt's uses the same cut.

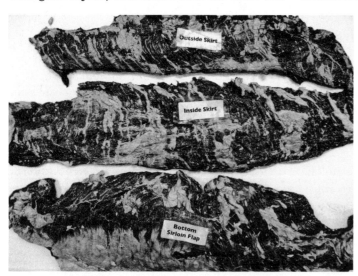

BOTTOM SIRLOIN flap, inside skirt steak, and outside skirt steak are similar-looking cuts

"We use beef tenderloins," she said. "We brush the meat with our Black Magic sauce when it comes off the grill—and that's it." The tenderloin they were talking about wasn't the Prime or Choice stuff you eat in fancy steak houses.

Below USDA Prime, Choice, and Select, there are the USDA Standard, Commercial, Utility, and Canner grades. You never see these in restaurants or grocery stores, but that doesn't mean you aren't eating them. USDA inspection is mandatory for all meat plants. Most people assume this means all meat is graded—but it's not. USDA grading is a service that meat processors can elect to pay extra for. And it costs a lot of money.

A Prime, Choice, or Select grade brings a bonus price; lesser grades don't add anything to the bottom line. Meat packers don't waste money getting older or less muscled steers graded. But the meat still gets sold. It's called ungraded beef. Ungraded tenderloin, known as cow tenders in the meat trade, is relatively cheap compared to USDA Choice inside skirt steak. Meat quality is not as simple as the labels make it seem.

In our final day of Beef 101, we sat in a classroom eating little chunks of beef in plastic cups and rating them on a one-to-ten scale for a variety of sensory evaluation factors including juiciness, tenderness, and overall impression. We checked off flavor notes on a list that included fatty, bloody, livery, grassy, soda, salt, chemical, bitter, soapy, metallic, and a taste researchers describe as "cardboard."

The first thing that became apparent as we raised our hands to vote for sample A or sample B was that we all had different tastes in beef. The class compared Select to Choice and Prime, wet-aged to dry-aged, grass-fed to grain-fed, and Angus to Charolais and Brahman genetics. We assessed the palatability of beef—which was stripped of labels, prejudices, and romantic steak house ambiance—like meat scientists.

The results were surprising. The vast majority of the class preferred wet-aged beef, despite the exalted reputa-

ALWAYS A FORT Worth favorite, Joe T. Garcia's opened in 1935

tion of expensive dry-aging. And a USDA Prime rib-eye sample was scored lower by most of the class on overall impression than one particular piece of USDA Choice.

The recession hurt luxury steak houses and raised demand for cheaper beef cuts. But a lot of consumers and restaurant chefs had already tired of big steaks anyway. "I love secondary cuts; choice tenderloin is boring," Mark Mavrantonis said. "There's a lot more character in brisket, short ribs, skirts, and some of these other new cuts."

Tenderloin or fajitas? Prime, Choice, or Select? I used to put a lot of faith in those names, whether I encountered them in restaurants or on the Styrene packages of meat in the grocery store. Now I know better.

When I started testing fajitas, I let flavor and tenderness be my guide. For the inside skirt steak, I bought marinated meats at Mexican carnicerias. But I also adapted some of the new bistro steak cuts to the backyard grill. I think you'll find some of these "new fajitas" interesting.

Tex-Mex Fajita Marinade

MAKES 4½ CUPS

PINEAPPLE JUICE AND SOY SAUCE ARE THE BASIS OF THE STAN-
dard Tex-Mex restaurant fajita marinade. It makes measuring easy if you start
with a whole bottle of soy sauce. You need about a cup for each pound of meat.

 2 cups pineapple juice
 2 cups (or one 500-milliliter bottle) soy sauce
 3 limes
 4 cloves garlic, minced

Combine the pineapple juice and soy sauce in a large mixing bowl. Wash the
limes and zest them, adding the lime zest to the juice and soy sauce mixture.
Cut the limes in half after zesting and squeeze the juice into the bowl. Throw
the lime halves in the bowl, too. Add the garlic. Use as a marinade.

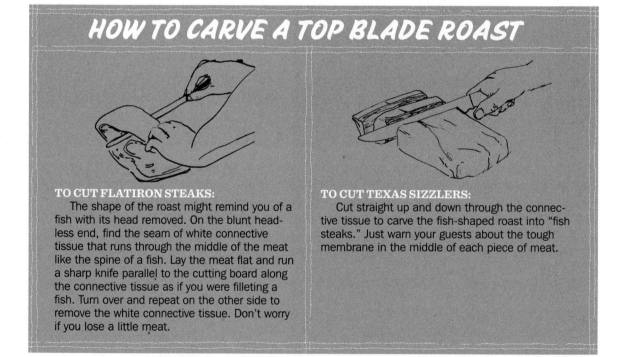

HOW TO CARVE A TOP BLADE ROAST

TO CUT FLATIRON STEAKS:
 The shape of the roast might remind you of a
fish with its head removed. On the blunt head-
less end, find the seam of white connective
tissue that runs through the middle of the meat
like the spine of a fish. Lay the meat flat and run
a sharp knife parallel to the cutting board along
the connective tissue as if you were filleting a
fish. Turn over and repeat on the other side to
remove the white connective tissue. Don't worry
if you lose a little meat.

TO CUT TEXAS SIZZLERS:
 Cut straight up and down through the connective tissue to carve the fish-shaped roast into "fish
steaks." Just warn your guests about the tough
membrane in the middle of each piece of meat.

Flatiron Fajitas

SERVES 2 TO 3

IF YOU CAN FIND FLATIRON STEAKS IN YOUR MEAT MARKET, you can start with those. If not, buy a "beef chuck top blade roast" and cut your own. The top blade yields wonderfully tender pieces of meat that are difficult to portion as steaks—but they lend themselves perfectly to fajitas.

    1 pound flatiron steaks or 1.3 to 1.5 pounds beef chuck top blade roast
    2 cups Tex-Mex Fajita Marinade (page 66)
    Salt and pepper
    1 lime
    Fajita Fixin's (see below)

Put the flatiron steaks in a resealable plastic bag with the fajita marinade and gently remove the air. Place the bag in a bowl to catch any leakage and place it in the refrigerator for a couple of hours.

Light the grill (preferably with mesquite). Put the meat on the hot part of the grill and cook, turning once or twice, until it reaches an internal temperature of 140° F for medium-rare. The meat is very tender; you don't need to overcook it. Remove from the grill and salt and pepper to taste.

Cut a test slice to find the direction of the grain, then cut into thin strips against the grain. Squeeze the lime over the meat and serve immediately with warm flour tortillas and other fajita fixin's.

VARIATION
NAKED FLATIRON FAJITAS
Omit the marinade.

FAJITA FIXIN'S

Mix and match your favorites to customize your fajita feast.
    Warm flour tortillas
    Guacamole (page 197)
    Refried Beans (page 204)
    Black Bean Hummus (page 74)
    Onions and Cilantro (page 169)
    Grilled onions
    Grilled peppers
    Salsas (see chapter 10) ·
    Chopped tomatoes
    Lime quarters
    Black olives

Butterflied Tri-Tip Fajitas

SERVES 4 TO 6

THE TRI-TIP ROAST IS EXTREMELY POPULAR FOR BARBECUE IN California. I like it even better double-butterflied into a flat piece of meat and soaked in Tex-Mex fajita marinade.

One 2- to 2½-pound tri-tip roast
4 cups Tex-Mex Fajita Marinade (page 66)
Salt and pepper
1 lime
Fajita Fixin's (page 67)

Rinse the roast and pat it dry. The roast is triangular in shape. Double-butterfly it one thin piece. (See How to Butterfly, below.)

Put the whole piece of meat in a resealable gallon-size plastic bag with the fajita marinade and gently remove the air. Place the bag in a bowl to catch any leakage and place it in the refrigerator for a couple of hours.

Light the grill (preferably with mesquite). Put the meat on the hot part of the grill and cook, turning once or twice, until it reaches an internal temperature of 145° F for medium. Remove from the grill and salt and pepper to taste.

Cut a test slice to find the direction of the grain, then cut into thin strips against the grain. Squeeze the lime over the meat and serve immediately with warm flour tortillas and other fajita fixin's.

HOW TO BUTTERFLY

TO BUTTERFLY: Lay the meat on a cutting board and pretend it's a book that you are going to open so an equal number of pages end up on each side. Insert a sharp knife on the right side (the left if you're left-handed) and cut toward the other side, being careful not to cut through the

"spine." Lay the book open and push down on the spine to flatten.
TO DOUBLE BUTTERFLY: Repeat the process, starting at the middle of the book and cutting once in either direction to create a "fold-out section." You should end up with four flaps of meat.

Kalbi Fajitas

SERVES 2 TO 3

BONELESS SHORT-RIB MEAT, KNOWN AS *KALBI,* IS ONE OF TWO cuts made famous by Korean barbecue restaurants; the other is the thin-sliced rib eye called *bulgogi.*

I figured this would make interesting fajita meat, and it did—but it took some experimenting. First I sliced the meat too thick and it was too tough. Then I cut it too thin and the pieces were difficult to handle; some of them slithered through the grill.

Finally, I went to a Korean grocery store and bought precut kalbi meat to see how they did it. That's how I ended up with the neatly cut rectangles I specify here. If you find the meat too tough, cut it a little thinner than a quarter inch or pound it flat.

1 pound boneless chuck short rib
2 cups Tex-Mex Fajita Marinade (page 66)
Salt and pepper
1 lime
Fajita Fixin's (page 67)

Cut the short-rib meat into rectangles 4½ inches long by 1½ inches wide by ¼ inch thick.

Put the meat in a resealable plastic bag with the fajita marinade and gently remove the air. Place the bag in a bowl to catch any leakage and leave it in the refrigerator for a couple of hours.

Light the grill (preferably with mesquite). Put the meat on the hot part of the grill and cook, turning once or twice, until it gets nicely charred. Remove from the grill and salt and pepper to taste.

Squeeze the lime over the meat and serve immediately with warm flour tortillas and other fajita fixin's.

THE FAJITAS at Original Ninfa's on Navigation in Houston are made with certified Hereford outside skirt steak

Viet-Mex Fajita Rolls

SERVES 4

AT MATT'S RANCHO MARTINEZ IN DALLAS, THEY HAVE AN APPE-
tizer called fried avocados. The deep-fried wedges are served with romaine
lettuce "taco shells," cilantro, slivers of carrots and jicama, and other fixin's.

"I got the idea from Vietnamese restaurants," said Marco Martinez, son of
the late Matt Martinez Jr. "The lettuce rolls are great for people on the Atkins
diet, too; they put their fajitas on them. We use soy sauce on the fajitas—we
borrow lots of thing from Asian cooking."

Making Viet-Mex salad rolls is sort of like making lettuce tacos. Put all the
ingredients out on the table and let everybody "roll their own."

2 pounds grilled fajita meat of your choice,
   sliced in thin strips
1 cup cilantro sprigs
1 large tomato, chopped
1 avocado, peeled and sliced
4 green onions, chopped
½ cup thin-sliced raw carrot strips
½ cup thin-sliced jicama strips
¼ cup dry-roasted peanuts, chopped
2 limes, cut into wedges
1 head of romaine lettuce, washed and dried,
   for wrappers
1 cup salsa of your choice

Put hot sliced beef on a platter surrounded by the cilantro, tomato, avocado, green onions, carrots, jicama, peanuts, and limes. Use lettuce leaves
to roll up steak slices with the other ingredients. Drizzle with lime juice
just before serving.

Leb-Mex Fajitas

MAKES 12 PITA WRAPS

THE KARAMS OF SAN ANTONIO AND THE JOSEPHS OF AUSTIN are two Lebanese-Texan families who started famous Tex-Mex restaurants. Middle Eastern and Mexican culture have long overlapped in Texas. Jalapeño falafels, black bean hummus, and salsa-drenched shawarmas are old hat in Houston. Lebanese immigrants have made significant contributions to Mexican cuisine, too. The vertical roaster used to make tacos al pastor was originally taken to Mexico to make shawarmas. The famous *tacos arabes* of Puebla are served on thick pita-like flatbreads. So it's not much of a stretch to substitute black bean hummus for refried beans and pita bread for flour tortillas when you're eating fajitas. Besides, fast-food restaurants have been selling "fajita pitas" for years.

> 6 large or 12 small pita bread rounds
> 3 pounds grilled fajita meat of your choice, sliced into thin strips
> Lime wedges
> Black Bean Hummus (page 74)
> Onions and Cilantro (page 169)
> 1 tomato, chopped
> Black olives

Heat the pita bread on the grill while you're cooking the fajitas. Put the hot sliced beef on a platter garnished with lime wedges. Serve the hummus, Onions and Cilantro, tomato, and olives in bowls on the table. Use pieces of pita to roll up fajitas with the other ingredients.

FAJITAS, CARNE ASADA, AND TACOS AL CARBON

Carne asada is the name used in Sonora and the West Coast of the United States to describe inexpensive beef cuts, such as skirt steak, rump, or sirloin flap, which have been grilled and chopped into thin strips. In Texas, the same cuts are called fajitas, regardless of whether or not they came from a skirt steak. *Tacos al carbon,* which once meant beef cooked over charcoal, is now used to describe gas-grill beef tacos too.

Black Bean Hummus

Makes 4 cups

THIS CHILLED BEAN MIXTURE IS A WELCOME CHANGE FOR summer fajita dinners. The flavor will remind you of Tex-Mex refried beans, but substituting olive oil and tahini for the lard makes for a lighter and fresher taco.

2 cups cooked black beans, drained and rinsed (one 20-ounce can)
½ cup tahini
½ cup freshly squeezed lemon juice
¼ cup fresh cilantro leaves
¼ cup chopped green onion
3 cloves garlic
¼ cup olive oil
1 teaspoon ground cumin
1 teaspoon powdered chile (page 233)
Tabasco or other hot sauce, to taste
Salt to taste

Puree all ingredients in a food processor until smooth. If the mixture is too thick, add more lemon juice and olive oil. Season to taste and refrigerate.

Classic Fajitas

Serves 2 to 3

THIS IS THE WAY SONNY FALCON USED TO MAKE IT. HE NEVER marinated the meat; it was simply trimmed of connective tissue, butterflied (see page 68), grilled, and then chopped against the grain into bite-size pieces. Be careful: the grain of the meat runs sideways, not lengthwise.

1 pound outside skirt steak
Salt and pepper
Warm flour tortillas
1 lime
Fajita Fixin's (page 67)

Heat the grill. Using a sharp knife, remove any membrane or silver skin and butterfly each flap. Grill over a hot fire for 12 to 15 minutes, or until well done. Salt and pepper to taste. Transfer to a cutting board and cut the length into 4-inch pieces, then turn it sideways to chop against the grain into strips. Divide the meat among the tortillas and sprinkle with lime juice just before serving. Pass fajita fixin's at the table.

Mole-Crusted Fajitas

SERVES 4

YOU'D THINK THE MOLE WOULD BURN UP AND TURN BLACK, but in fact, it creates a wonderful crust. This easy recipe is adapted from a much more elaborate recipe that Chef Robert Del Grande came up with many years ago. He made the mole from scratch.

- 2 pounds sirloin flap
- 6 tablespoons commercial mole (such as Doña Maria)
- 1 tablespoon chunky peanut butter
- ¼ cup peanut oil
- 2 cloves garlic, minced
- Salt
- Ancho-Raisin Salsa (page 226)

Clean the flap meat of connective tissue, rinse, and set aside. In a mixing bowl, combine the mole, peanut butter, peanut oil, and garlic. Stir until the lumps dissolve. Rub the marinade all over the beef and allow to stand for about 30 minutes. Light the grill. Grill the beef, but don't overcook it. The meat should be slightly pink. Slice extremely thin. Salt to taste. Spoon salsa over the meat and serve immediately.

OUTSIDE SKIRT, THE ORIGINAL FAJITA MEAT

Outside skirt steak still exists, of course. It's just hard to get. If you want to go to the trouble, you can order outside skirt steak at a good butchershop. If you do, you might as well specify USDA Choice, Certified Angus Beef, or Certified Hereford Beef.

A MEXICAN *TAQUERO* grilling on mesquite coals in a sawed-in-half 55-gallon barrel at the Monterrey *tianguis*

#4

MEAT AND BEER IN MONTERREY

EL INDIO AZTECA IS A LEGENDARY MONTERREY BAR. It's decorated with dark wood paneling and lots of deer heads. The *taverna muy famosa* recently celebrated its hundredth anniversary. • "What's your specialty?" I asked the third-generation proprietor, Felipe González González, as I looked over the menu. • "We have only meat," he replied. I had to chuckle at his response. "Regios," as the people of Monterrey are called, are unabashed carnivores. They eat meat for breakfast, lunch, and dinner and they don't see anything unusual about it. All that meat goes great with their other obsession: beer.

Monterrey is home to Cervecería Cuauhtémoc Moctezuma, Mexico's largest brewery. They are the makers of such popular brands as Dos Equis, Tecate, and Bohemia and Mexican favorites Carta Blanca and Indio. When you go drinking in Monterrey, don't make the mistake I did and ask for Negra Modelo; that brand, along with Corona, is made by Mexico's second largest brewery, Grupo Modelo—a bitter rival based in Mexico City.

Beer is the beverage of choice at El Indio Azteca and in the old days, the *botanas*, or bar snacks, were free. With your first round, you got a small plate, and with your second you got something bigger. The more you drank, the better the botanas would get. Luckily, you don't have to drink your way to the quality chow anymore; you just order whatever you like from the menu.

A side dish of roasted serrano chiles with lots of black char and lime wedges is set on the table with every dish. There's a light coat of oil clinging to the serranos and they have been well salted. The roasting renders the peppers nearly heat-free. I ended up eating three with my first Bohemia. I

made a mental note to start roasting chiles every time I heat up the grill.

My drinking companion, Guillermo González Beristáin, recommended the *higado,* or pig's liver. Trained at the Culinary Institute of America, young, handsome, and six feet four inches tall, Guillermo is one of Mexico's top chefs. I met him at a culinary event in San Antonio and he invited me to look him up if I was ever in Monterrey.

While I was working on this book, I visited La Catarina, one of Guillermo's restaurants. He taught me a little about cooking cabrito. When Guillermo got off work, we stopped by El Indio Azteca for a couple of cold ones and a chat about meat.

"So why is it that people eat so much meat in Monterrey?" I asked Guillermo as we chowed down. The chef's family came from Mexico City and he grew up in Ensenada, he explained, so he is not a local expert. But he does know a little about Mexico's food history.

The sparse vegetation of the desert Norteño region supports livestock grazing, but very little agriculture. For most of its history, Monterrey had only five

TEQUILA, SANGRITA,
and cold Superior
beer at El Indio
Azteca in Monterrey

staples besides meat, Guillermo observed: nopales ("cactus paddles"), tomatoes, chiles, tortillas, and beans. But while meat was considered a luxury in the rest of Mexico, here in the ranching region, it was among the cheapest foods available. The explanation makes a lot of sense—on both sides of the border.

The ranching culture of Northern Mexico is a window on the origins of Tex-Mex. Much has been made lately of "eating local." When you live in a cattle-raising center, eating local means eating meat.

ONE OF THE CLASSIEST MEAT MARkets in Monterrey is called Carnes Ramos, and it's located in the upscale San Pedro Garza Garcia neighborhood. Above the counter, there are food porn shots of steaks and roasts. The gigantic store is gleaming white, well scrubbed, and tastefully decorated, with faux marble floors. I stood in the middle of the butcher shop with a friend polishing off a half pound of hot chicharrones. The meat displayed here is in huge primal cuts, but in the end, people take it home in little plastic packages, just like we do in the United States.

CHEF GUILLERMO González Beristáin

One Friday night, Guillermo invited me to his home for an elegant dinner party. He and his gorgeous wife, Karina, live on the top of a mountain overlooking the city near Chipinque National Park. The menu included *cabrito en salsa,* a braised goat dish (see the similar recipe on page 104), *cabrito al pastor* grilled over mesquite (see the recipe on page 87), and *asado de puerco,* a pork dish with ancho and orange zest (see the recipe on page 108). We also had a red wine from Baja California that was bottled exclusively for Guillermo's restaurants.

Guillermo got his meat from restaurant suppliers, but he said that people who cooked cabrito at home in Monterrey prefer to buy their goats from local ranchers. Some drive out to the goat farms in the country, and some meet the ranchers at the *tianguis*—the local equivalent of a farmer's market.

The next morning, I grabbed a taxi and headed to the Saturday tianguis at Monterrey's abandoned train station. *Tianguis* is a Nahuatl word that means an impromptu market. This tianguis was a wild bazaar of fruits, vegetables, live animals, and most of all, fresh *carnes*.

I figured it would be a good place to study Norteño grilling firsthand, and I was not disappointed. There were grills and flat tops set up everywhere. Each cook supervised an impromptu restaurant comprised of card tables and folding chairs surrounding the grill. Some were tiny affairs with a few customers and some were twenty-table operations.

The range in cooking equipment was staggering. A guy in a cowboy hat was grilling with mesquite wood on a fifty-five-gallon barrel "Texas hibachi" just like mine. This vaquero's customers were eating steaks, chicken pieces, sausage, and several other grilled cuts. I was interested to see him heating tortillas the way a hamburger joint in the United States heats hamburger buns—by stacking them on top of the grilling meat.

Another man was slow-cooking a cabrito and a whole pig in a giant *caja china,* the kind of slow cooker that was made popular by food vendors along the beaches of Puerto Rico. (For more about the caja china, see page 120.) I also saw a few food stalls where the beans and *nopalitos* and other dishes were cooked over charcoal on an old-fashioned brazier.

But by far the most common cooking fuel was propane. The cooking surfaces were split evenly between flat tops and grates. I saw small girls flipping tortillas, formidable women caramelizing onions and peppers, and lots of people making tacos on flat tops. Meanwhile on the gas grills with grates, all manner of meat was being cooked along with corn on the cob, chile peppers, and other food that needed to char.

A few stalls were devoted to fresh vegetables. I saw lots of nopales cactus pads and found mounds of wild chile pequíns for sale. But more than half of the stalls were devoted to meat.

In a beef-draped stall, a seated butcher carved paper-thin round steak slices for *milanesa* from a

CABRITO **STALL** at the Monterrey *tianguis*

huge hind leg of beef. He was surrounded by steaks, ribs, and skirts. A man walked by dragging a squealing live pig by the back leg, while at another stall, a guy in a cowboy hat stood frying chicharrones in beautiful copper vats. Freshly slaughtered kid goats hung from the awnings of several outdoor stalls. Passersby admired the pale, butter-colored flesh of the tiny carcasses, which were splayed open to show the kidneys still attached to ribs. Some of the dressed baby goats appeared to weigh less than six pounds.

Beneath the fresh meat display, a little chicken-wire pen held a dozen or so live kid goats. Regios like to develop a relationship with a rancher, my friend told me. Regular customers are invited to go visit the ranch and pay for their cabritos in advance and specify how they will be fed and at what age they will be killed. Then they meet the rancher at the market to inspect the animals and have them slaughtered on the spot.

It's a very enlightened way to buy meat—once you come to terms with your decision to eat baby goats. The animals are very cute and it's tough to remember that this isn't a petting zoo. The connoisseur's preference for ever smaller cabritos is easy to understand when the delicate milk-fed meat is on your plate. Here, you have to look the little fellows in the eyes, though. Like most Americans, I tend to think of baby animals as pets. The Saturday tianguis in Monterrey is a good place to get over that notion.

Monterrey is no little ranching town. It has become Mexico's most advanced city, with more universities and computers per capita than anywhere else in the country. And yet the people of Monterrey have never lost touch with their Norteño livestock-raising heritage. I envy the Regios for that—and for their easygoing love affair with meat.

Grilled Rib Eye with Chile Butter

SERVES 4

THROWING A STEAK ON THE FIRE IS GRILLING AT ITS MOST basic. How do you tell when it's done? Seven minutes on each side is a good guess for medium if you're cooking a half-inch-thick steak. Or you can use the "face touch" method (if it feels like your cheek it's rare, chin is medium, forehead is well-done). I used those methods most of my life and cursed myself when the meat came out overdone or underdone. Now I use a meat thermometer; 135°F is medium-rare, 140°F is medium.

In Monterrey, cheap grass-fed beef is the norm. It's cut into thin steaks and cooked well-done because it's tough. Expensive restaurants there serve thick-cut steaks of tender American grain-fed beef. Meanwhile, more and more Americans are paying a premium for grass-fed beef raised without chemicals.

> 4 rib-eye steaks, about 14 ounces each
> 4 teaspoons Tex-Mex Grill Blend (page 21)
> 4 round slices of Chile Butter (page 22)

Rub the steaks with Tex-Mex Grill Blend and allow to marinate in the refrigerator for several hours. Light the grill and let it get hot. Place the steaks on the grill and let them sit in the same place for 5 minutes while they develop a nice-looking grill mark. Repeat on the other side. Then place the steaks on a cooler part of the grill to finish cooking. This will allow the meat to cook evenly through the middle. For medium-rare, remove the steaks when they reach 135°F; for medium, 140°F. Top each steak with a cold slice of Chile Butter and serve immediately.

STEAK GRADES

Kobe (left) is the highly marbled beef of Japanese Waygu cattle. These cattle are now being raised in the United States, but there is no American grading system available. The Japanese beef grading system has several levels above the equivalent of USDA Prime.

USDA Prime (middle) is the highest attainable American beef grade. While dry-aged USDA Prime was once the chef's pick for the best quality steaks, Kobe cuts are now the most expensive in top steak houses.

USDA Choice (right) is a very broad category. Branded meat programs, such as Certified Angus, Certified Hereford, and Sterling Beef, cherry-pick the best cuts in the Choice category that meet their criteria to provide consumers with better steaks.

BIG DEAL MEALS

If you grill for a crowd, eventually you'll find yourself considering the merits of buying whole roasts and cutting them up. Working with larger cuts of meat is a little more work, but it's a lot less expensive. You can buy a whole rib roast and cut your own rib-eye steaks for a fraction of what you'd pay for the steaks sold separately. And there are some wonderful cuts, like Tex-Mex Churrasco (page 90), that just aren't available in the store. Here are a couple of recipes that require a little meat-cutting skill or some help from a butcher.

MEXICAN BUTCHER cutting steaks at the Monterrey *tianguis*

YOU CAN find leg of
goat steaks at halal
butcher shops

Leg-of-Goat Steaks with Honey-Habanero Glaze

MAKES FOUR ¼-POUND CHOPS

UNLESS YOU HAVE A BAND SAW AT HOME, you'll have to get the butcher to help you cut up a leg of goat—but it's well worth the trouble. Cabritos are popular in northern Mexico, but in Guadalajara and in Arab cultures, full-grown goat is more popular. The leg is the meatiest cut. Leg-of-goat steaks are surprisingly tender. I buy whole legs at a halal meat market and ask the butcher to cut them into steaks. A whole leg will yield seven or eight thin steaks and a lot of smaller chunks that are great for kebabs or ground meat.

> 4 goat leg steaks (about 1 pound total)
> 1 tablespoon olive oil
> 4 teaspoons Tex-Mex Grill Blend (page 21)
> 2 tablespoons butter
> ½ cup honey
> 1 habanero pepper

Rub the steaks with olive oil and then with the seasoning mix and allow to marinate in the refrigerator for a few hours. Light the grill (preferably with mesquite charcoal or mesquite wood burnt down to coals).

In a saucepan on the grill, melt the butter and dissolve the honey and bring to a simmer. Cut the habanero in half and drop it in the honey mixture. For a mild habanero flavor, remove the pepper after a few minutes and discard. For a medium habanero flavor with a noticeable picante buzz, remove the pepper after 5 or 6 minutes of simmering. For an intense habanero heat, leave the pepper in the glaze until it's ready to use.

Cook the steaks over high heat for 3 to 5 minutes or until nicely browned. Turn and cook on the other side. When nearly done to your liking, brush both sides with the honey-habanero glaze and turn a few times until the glaze bubbles; don't allow it to burn. Don't overcook the chops; they should be slightly pink and yield to the touch.

Rack of Lamb with Pepper Jelly Glaze

MAKES 8 SINGLE RIB CHOPS

RACK OF LAMB IS AN ELEGANT DINNER, BUT THE SIZE OF THE chops varies widely. You'll find that the big racks at some upscale butcher shops are rather expensive, while small racks of New Zealand lamb that weigh little more than a pound are often available at discount stores at very reasonable prices. You can use the same amount of marinade and glaze for one big rack or two tiny ones. A high-heat hardwood charcoal is a good choice for this kind of quick grilling.

    2 tablespoons olive oil
    1 tablespoon fresh rosemary leaves
    2 cloves garlic, chopped
    Whole rack of lamb chops
    2 teaspoons freshly squeezed lime juice
    4 tablespoons pepper jelly
    Sea salt
    1 tablespoon freshly ground black pepper

Combine the olive oil, rosemary, and garlic in a bowl and stir. Place the lamb in the marinade for at least 2 hours. In a small saucepan, combine the lime juice and pepper jelly.

Prepare a grill. Place the saucepan with the pepper jelly and lime juice on the grill and stir the mixture to dissolve the jelly. Remove the rack from the marinade and season with salt and pepper. Place the rack above high heat and cook bone side down for 3 minutes. Turn the rack, brush the meaty side with the pepper jelly glaze, and cook over high heat for another 2 minutes. Move to a cooler part of the grill and cook to 140°F internal temperature. Allow to rest for a few minutes, then carve into individual chops.

Grilled Cabrito

SERVES 4 TO 6

THIS RECIPE MAY SOUND DECEPTIVELY SIMPLE, BUT GREAT cabrito isn't the easiest thing to prepare. The secret is getting a freshly killed animal. Goat quickly develops a gamy aroma, so defrosting a frozen cabrito or buying a fresh cabrito a few days in advance and storing it in the fridge is a bad idea. Regios meet the goat rancher at the farmer's market and get their cabritos slaughtered a few hours before they intend to cook them. The closer you can get to this ideal, the better your cabrito will taste.

This recipe works best in a barrel smoker (Texas hibachi) with at least two feet by three feet of grill surface. If you are using a smaller grill, you will have to cut the animal up.

> 5 tablespoons salt
> 1 cup white vinegar
> 6- to 8-pound cabrito on the bone
> Olive oil
> 1 tablespoon sea salt
> 1 teaspoon freshly ground black pepper

Compare the dimensions of your grill with the size of the cabrito and decide if you can cook it whole. If not, cut the cabrito in quarters. Fill a clean laundry tub large enough to accommodate the cabrito with warm water and add the salt and vinegar. Wash the cabrito and allow it to soak while you prepare a mesquite fire.

Make a basting mop by mixing the olive oil, sea salt, and pepper with 2 cups of warm water. When the mesquite has burnt off and only coals remain, put the cabrito on the grill at least 18 inches above glowing coals. Grill for 2 hours, basting frequently and turning until all sides are golden brown. The meat should be white and juicy in the middle.

TEX-MEX RESTAURANT scion
Victor Leál—with his grilled
butterflied leg of lamb—in
his backyard, overlooking
the Palo Duro Canyon

Victor Leál's Leg of Lamb

SERVES 6

VICTOR LEÁL IS THE FORMER MAYOR OF MULESHOE. HIS FAMILY owns the Leál's tortilla factory there and a six-store chain of family restaurants. Victor currently owns and operates the Leál's in Amarillo, one of the most innovative Tex-Mex restaurants in the state. (Don't miss the avocado enchiladas if you go.) When I asked Victor what he liked to grill, he invited me over to his house, where he did this butterflied leg of lamb on a Weber in the backyard. The rosemary was cut from bushes in his yard. And since his backyard overlooks the Palo Duro Canyon, it was a pretty spectacular dinner. We had the lamb with grilled pineapple and an excellent red wine at an elegantly set table outside on the patio.

½ leg of lamb, butterflied (about 3 pounds)

ROSEMARY RUB
½ cup fresh rosemary leaves
5 cloves garlic
1 bunch of green onions, coarsely chopped
Juice of 1 lime
¼ cup peanut oil
1 jalapeño pepper, stemmed and seeded
1 tablespoon cracked black pepper
2 teaspoons sea salt

Spread the butterflied roast on a cutting board. Beat the large clumps of meat with a tenderizing hammer to soften but be careful not to separate the pieces from each other. Turn and beat the other side. Spread plastic wrap over the softened meat and with the broad side of a meat cleaver flatten the roast out until it is roughly about as thick as a steak.

Combine the rub ingredients in a food processor and pulse until the mixture forms a thick paste. Lay the meat on a piece of plastic wrap large enough to wrap it. Rub the paste into the meat, then roll the meat up and spread more paste onto the other side as you wrap it up. Allow to marinate in the refrigerator for several hours. Remove from the refrigerator 30 minutes in advance of cooking and unroll.

Light a grill. Over medium-high heat, cook the flattened roast as if it were a steak, about 7 minutes on each side for medium or to an internal temperature of 140°F at the thickest spot. With a slicing knife, carve on the diagonal into ¼-inch-thick strips, discarding ligament and connective tissue as you carve. Serve with Refried Black Beans (page 204) and Chile Grilled Pineapple (page 208.)

GRILLING STEAKS is elevated to an art form at the annual Texas Steak Cook-Off in Hico

Tex-Mex Churrasco

SERVES 8

CHURRASCO IS A WORD WITH MANY MEANINGS. IN BRAZIL, IT IS the general term for grilled meat, and a churrascaría is a Brazilian steak house. In Argentina, churrasco means skirt steak. But in Nicaragua, a churrasco is a beef tenderloin cut into thin slices and grilled, usually served with chimichurri sauce. The Nicaraguan style of churrasco has became famous in the Latino communities of Texas and Florida, and that's what we're cooking here.

Beef tenderloin, cleaned and peeled, about 4 pounds
Tex-Mex Chimichurri (recipe follows)

This technique is similar to butterflying (see page 68). But instead of cutting the meat into connected pieces, you are going to cut it all the way through. Place the tenderloin on a cutting board. With a sharp knife, remove any remaining silver skin. Holding the knife parallel to the cutting board, split the log of meat lengthwise into 2 long half logs. Now slice each of these in half again to form 4 long, thin slices.

Turn the knife the other way and cut each thin slice in half to make 8 shorter pieces. Cover each with plastic wrap and pound them flat with the broad side of a meat clever. The meat is soft, so don't overdo it. Remove the plastic wrap and put the flattened tenderloin pieces in a baking dish, coating each with a little chimichurri sauce and pouring more over the top. Allow to marinate for an hour or so in the refrigerator.

Light the grill. Remove the meat from the refrigerator. Place cold slices of meat on the hot grill, turning after a minute or so. Don't bother trying to check the temperature with a thermometer—the meat isn't thick enough. Check doneness by cutting into a piece, but you'd better move fast because it will only take 3 to 4 minutes for medium-rare.

Serve the meat with the chimichurri sauce, grilled corn, cold sliced tomatoes, and green salad in the summer. In the winter, you might serve it with baked potatoes.

Tex-Mex Chimichurri

MAKES ABOUT 1½ CUPS

THE ORIGINAL CHIMICHURRI OF ARGENTINA IS EATEN WITH grilled meats of all varieties. I've substituted cilantro and lime juice for the parsley and red wine vinegar of the South American version; you'll like the Tex-Mex version even better than the original.

1 cup fresh cilantro leaves
8 cloves garlic, minced
½ cup olive oil
½ cup freshly squeezed lime juice
1 tablespoon minced red onion
1 teaspoon freshly ground black pepper
½ teaspoon sea salt
½ teaspoon dried Mexican oregano

Place all of the ingredients in a blender. Pulse to combine, then blend until smooth. Will keep for a few days in the refrigerator.

HOW TO CUT A WHOLE TENDERLOIN

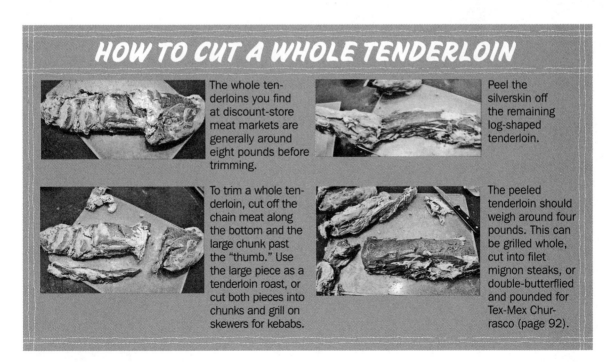

The whole tenderloins you find at discount-store meat markets are generally around eight pounds before trimming.

Peel the silverskin off the remaining log-shaped tenderloin.

To trim a whole tenderloin, cut off the chain meat along the bottom and the large chunk past the "thumb." Use the large piece as a tenderloin roast, or cut both pieces into chunks and grill on skewers for kebabs.

The peeled tenderloin should weigh around four pounds. This can be grilled whole, cut into filet mignon steaks, or double-butterflied and pounded for Tex-Mex Churrasco (page 92).

JOSÉ LUIS López
sells the best bar-
bacoa in Houston at
Gerardo's Drive-in
Grocery, on Patton

CHAPTER 5

BACKYARD BARBACOA AND SMOKE-BRAISING

IT WAS QUARTER TO ELEVEN ON SUNDAY MORNING IN HOUSton and the sidewalks in front of Gerardo's Drive-in Grocery on Patton were a street party. There were families carrying their food home in white paper bags and then there were the people who just couldn't wait. • One guy had opened up a container of barbacoa meat, some salsas, and a foil package of tortillas and lined them up along the window sill under the burglar bars where he stood making tacos. A couple of women were using the newspaper machines right outside the front door as stand-up counters for their coffee cups. It was all making me hungry.

GERARDO'S, BARBACOA, VI, SA, DO, read the sign out front. Which means that barbacoa is available on Friday (Viernes), Saturday (Sábado), and Sunday (Domingo) only. Ten years ago, that was standard policy. But these days, you see barbacoa and every other variety of Mexican street food offered 24/7 at taco trucks and gas-station taquerias all over the city. So how does Gerardo's still manage to draw such a crowd for their weekend specials, I wondered, as I shouldered my way inside. When I got up to the meat counter, my question was answered.

At other taquerias and carnicerias the "mystery meats" get a little crusty in the stainless-steel bins on the steam tables. You might have trouble finding something that looks appetizing. But at Gerardo's you have the opposite problem: all the meats look so good, you want to eat everything. And believe me, I tried.

I loved the dark brown Texas-style barbacoa, which was made from steamed cattle cabezas. Gerardo's steams the seasoned cow heads in giant gas-fired stainless-steel jacketed kettles that retain the broth. The gelatinous meat is satin slick on the tongue and tastes awesome with Gerardo's tart green tomatillo and serrano salsa. On a second weekend visit, two companions and I sat down at a table with a dozen fat tamales, a pound of barbacoa de borrego, a pile of tortillas, and assorted condiments.

The barbacoa de borrego was unique. The chunks of meat were falling-apart-tender and were served with a deep red chile broth. It reminded me of the stewed goat dish called *birria*. Gerardo López, who was working the meat counter that day, told me that they made the barbacoa de borrego with goat meat. That was confusing, since borrego means sheep or mutton. So I asked his father, José Luis López, for an explanation. (The store is named for Gerardo López, but it's owned by his parents, José Luis and Maria López.)

"We make the barbacoa de borrego with lamb shoulder and goat meat, mixed half and half, then seasoned with garlic, bay leaves, oregano, and chili powder," José Luis said. The meats are cooked slowly for twelve hours in the steam kettle. Then the meat is stripped from the bone, shredded, and steeped in the broth. It's really a cross between the Mexican goat stewed in chile broth called birria and maguey-leaf-wrapped barbacoa de borrego. The meat is absolutely fabulous—if you like that kind of thing.

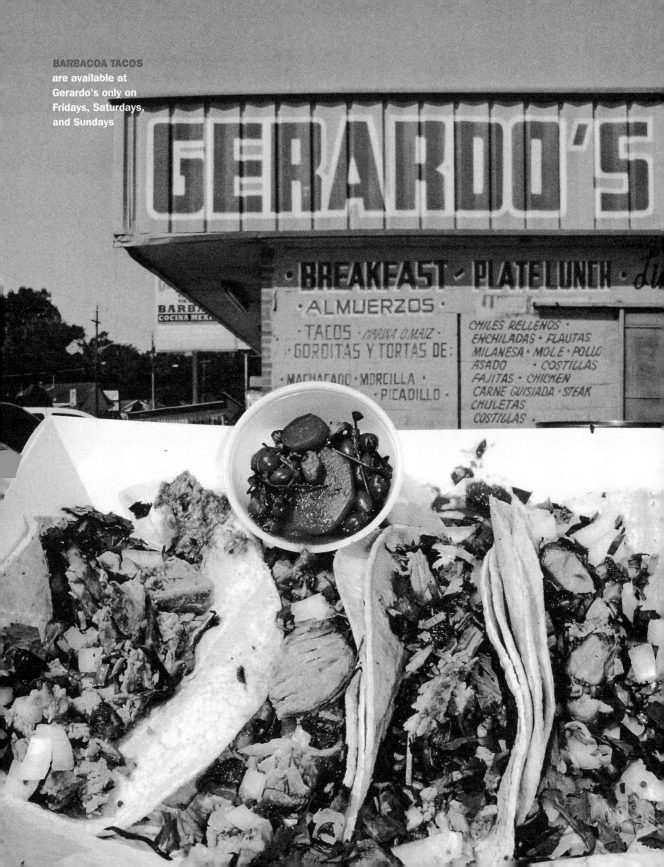

BARBACOA TACOS are available at Gerardo's only on Fridays, Saturdays, and Sundays

"I can't get over that wet dog aroma," one of my tablemates said after trying to eat some on a taco. Some people like mutton and goat, and some don't.

I guess I like wet dogs, because I couldn't get enough borrego tacos, which I made on corn tortillas with the spicy meat and the pickled chile pequíns that Gerardo's offers alongside the salsas. It's nice to see chile pequíns as a condiment selection. They are the traditional peppers of southern Texas and northern Mexico, and the tiny round chiles still grow wild in vacant lots and along fence rows all over the city. The ones you see in stores are harvested by hand in wilderness areas in Sonora. You find them in farmer's markets and meat markets like Gerardo's in the autumn. And they are usually the most expensive chile peppers you can buy.

José Luis, who was born in Michoacán, opened the business as a corner grocery in 1977, so I guess he has had some time to practice. The grocery still offers a few raw vegetables and some raw meats along with the soft drinks and the chips, but mostly people come for Gerardo's cooking.

Weekend mornings are the most fun, but Gerardo's also serves breakfast specials and plate lunches Monday through Friday. I stopped by for lunch on a recent Monday afternoon around one o'clock and had the place pretty much to myself.

I had a plate of carne asada in a dark red sauce. In Mexico, *carne asada* or *asado del puerco* means braised pork. Gerardo's is a slow-roasted pork shoulder in an intense sauce of garlic and dried ancho chiles, seasoned with what tastes like orange

THE MEANING OF BARBACOA

The English word *barbecue* is derived from the Spanish word *barbacoa*. There are lots of varieties of barbacoa in Mexico. The world's largest Mexican restaurant, Arroyo in Mexico City, has made its style of *barbacoa de borrego* (barbecued lamb) famous. At the authentic Huastecan restaurant called El Hidalguense in Houston, barbacoa means lamb shoulder sealed in maguey leaves and cooked in the coals of a wood fire.

Tex-Mex barbacoa is almost always made from *cabeza de la vaca,* or cow head. Cow heads became the most popular meat for barbacoa in Texas because Latino ranch hands were given cow heads as part of their pay. If you ever saw the movie *Giant,* you might remember Elizabeth Taylor fainting when the vaqueros unwrapped the burlap bag containing the head that had been buried under the coals.

Today, the barbacoa found in Tex-Mex restaurants is usually made from seasoned cow heads that are steamed in an oven with a *baño maria* (bain-marie) or in a steam-jacketed kettle. There are very few old-fashioned barbacoa pits left in Texas; a restaurant called Vera's in Brownsville is the only one I have seen. Modern health department regulations have pretty much put an end to authentic pit barbacoa.

THIS *BARBACOA de borrego* is made from a lamb shoulder roast that's smoke-braised until it's falling-apart tender

peel and bay leaves. The chile sauce is cooked down until it's almost black—but when you spread it on a tortilla, it turns a deep brick red. The carne asada at Gerardo's Drive-in Grocery was the best I have eaten in the United States.

A T TEX-MEX RESTAURANTS AND taquerias, cow heads are cooked in a steam-jacketed kettle like they have at Gerardo's, or in an oven with a baño Maria (bain-marie). At home, I have made an excellent recipe using an electric roasting oven.

But steamed meat doesn't fit the definition of barbecue for most American "Q" aficionados. And I must admit I have always wanted to cook barbacoa on a barbecue pit. So when I started writing this book, I began experimenting with braising on the grill.

My idea was to start out with the same ingredients they use to make barbacoa at Gerardo's, but add a smoking step and put the braising liquid on the grill. To get the falling-apart texture I wanted, I finished by wrapping the meat with aluminum foil—the way some people finish a barbecued brisket.

The cow head barbacoa came out fine, but it was a lot of trouble. A cow head is awfully big and would only fit on the very largest of grills. (I put it on my Big Ugly Barrel.) I can't say it was worth the effort. But the technique worked great.

So I tried the same concept with more manageable cuts like beef short ribs and pork asado, and I was blown away by the flavor. Any backyard barbecuer could follow these recipes on a Weber. I thought it was a momentous discovery until I noticed that my friend Bruce Aidells was publishing similar recipes, and a few Texas barbecuers reminded me that turning a brisket in a liquid on the smoker is a time-honored method. So I guess the truth is this new technique is as old as the hills; and it's also very labor intensive.

But if you are ready to take on the ultimate challenge in Tex-Mex grilling, you are going to love this "Backyard Barbacoa."

SMOKE-BRAISED short ribs are grilled in a pan

Beef Short Ribs in Ancho-Molasses Sauce

MAKES ABOUT 1½ POUNDS OF MEAT

THE KEY TO THIS RECIPE IS TO START THE RIBS IN A PAN; TURN-ing them in the melted tallow fat will crisp them up. It's like frying and smoking them at the same time. Let them get well-done before you add the hot braising liquid.

6 beef short ribs (square cut, around 3 pounds)
2 tablespoons Tex-Mex Grill Blend (page 21)
2 ancho chiles, stemmed and seeded
12-ounce can root beer (sweetened with cane sugar)
1 tablespoon vegetable oil
½ onion, chopped
3 cloves garlic, chopped
1 cup molasses

FOR SERVING
12 warm flour tortillas
Onions and Cilantro (see page 169)
2 cups Refried Beans (see page 204)

Light about 25 charcoal briquettes in a chimney and prepare the grill with the coals on one side only. Rub the ribs with the seasoning blend and place them in a pan. Put the pan on the grill over medium-hot coals and turn the ribs when they start to sizzle. Continue cooking in the dish for 1 hour, turning to caramel-ize on all sides. Move the pan to the cool side of the grill if the meat begins to burn or stick.

Tear the ancho chiles into pieces and combine with the root beer in a sauce-pan over medium heat. Simmer until the chiles soften, about 15 minutes. Heat the oil in a skillet and add the onion. Cook until softened, about 5 minutes. Add the garlic and cook for another minute. Add the root beer and chile mixture and bring to a boil, then reduce the heat to a simmer.

Add more wood and charcoal to the grill if needed. When the ribs are well browned, pour the molasses over each rib, turning to coat. Then add the hot root beer–chile mixture to the pan. Place the pan over hot coals so it simmers.

Cover the grill and allow the ribs to smoke and simmer for another hour, turning often. Cover the pan with aluminum foil and allow to steam for 30 min-utes. Remove the pan from the grill and put the ribs in a serving dish. Stir the braising liquid and molasses in the pan together and pour over the ribs. Serve immediately with the flour tortillas, Onions and Cilantro, and Refried Beans.

Barbacoa de Borrego

MAKES ABOUT 4 POUNDS OF MEAT

A SQUARE-CUT LAMB SHOULDER ROAST WORKS PERFECTLY FOR this and is fairly inexpensive, but unfortunately the cut is hard to find. Leg of lamb works, too, but it ain't cheap. At Gerardo's, the kitchen crew uses a half goat and half lamb mixture. Feel free to experiment.

Square-cut lamb shoulder roast, 7 to 8 pounds
2 tablespoons Tex-Mex Grill Blend (page 21)

FOR THE CHILE PUREE
2 ancho chiles, stemmed and seeded
2 guajillo chiles, stemmed and seeded
2 chipotle chiles, stemmed and seeded
   (or substitute available dried chiles)

FOR THE SAUCE
2 tablespoons olive oil
1 onion, chopped
2 celery stalks, cleaned and chopped
4 cloves garlic, minced
14.5-ounce can stewed tomatoes
2 carrots, peeled and chopped
Leaves from 3 sprigs fresh rosemary, cleaned and chopped
Leaves from 3 sprigs fresh thyme, cleaned and chopped
Salt and pepper

FOR SERVING
24 warm flour tortillas
Onions and Cilantro (page 169)
2 cups Refried Beans (page 204)
Chile Grilled Pineapple (page 208)

Rub the meat with the seasoning blend and allow it to marinate in the refrigerator for a few hours. Light about 25 charcoal briquettes in a chimney and prepare a grill with the coals on one side only. Brown the lamb roast over the hot fire for 10 to 15 minutes, turning often, until well browned. Move it to the cool side of the grill or to the smoking chamber of an offset barbecue smoker. Put some hardwood chips or chunks on the coals and close the lid. Allow the roast to smoke for 1½ to two hours at around 250°F, turning to cook evenly.

Meanwhile, make the puree: In a saucepan over low heat, simmer the chiles in water to cover. Allow them to sit in the hot water for 10 to 20 minutes until soft. Puree the chiles in a blender, adding the soaking water a little at a time until the puree is smooth.

Make the sauce: In a soup pot, heat the oil over medium heat and add the onion and celery. Stir and cook for 5 minutes. Add the garlic and cook another few minutes. Add the chile puree and cook for 3 minutes, stirring well. Add the remaining vegetables and herbs and 8 cups of water and bring the mixture to a boil. Turn down the heat and allow to simmer. Season to taste with salt and pepper.

Add more charcoal and wood to the fire. Place a large metal roasting pan on the grill directly over the coals. Carefully pour the chile sauce into the roasting pan. Place the meat in the roasting pan with the sauce. Allow the meat to simmer and smoke for 1 to 1½ hours, replenishing the liquid level with water if needed.

With the aid of fire gloves or pot holders, remove the pan from the fire and cover the roast and the roasting pan with aluminum foil and seal tightly. Return to the fire. Simmer over the coals or in a 300°F oven for another hour or two until the meat is extremely tender. You want the shape to be intact, but the meat to be very soft.

TO SERVE: Remove the meat from the sauce and allow to cool slightly. Reserve the sauce. Clean the meat away from the bones and chop lightly. Serve the cleaned meat in some chile sauce with more chile sauce on the side. You can also serve some of the sauce in a cup as a first course. Place the warm flour tortillas, warm Refried Beans, and Onions and Cilantro on the table. Allow your guests to make their own tacos.

STEP-BY-STEP BACKYARD barbacoa: 1. Season the roast. 2. Grill the roast while preparing a braising sauce. 3. Put a roasting pan full of the braising sauce on the grill. 4. Turn the roast in the sauce on the covered grill for a few hours. 5. Seal with aluminum foil and simmer until extremely tender.

Leg of Goat Barbacoa

MAKES ABOUT 2 POUNDS OF MEAT

FOR THIS RECIPE, YOU WANT A BIG MEATY GOAT LEG, NOT A little cabrito leg. Halal meat markets (which prepare meat according to Islamic law) are my favorite place to shop for this kind of goat. In Texas, halal meat markets sell the meaty Boer crossbreeds called "redheads."

2½- to 3-pound leg of goat
1 teaspoon garlic powder
1 teaspoon freshly ground black pepper
12 tomatillos, husked and rinsed, or 3 cups tomatillo puree
2 tablespoons olive oil
2 celery stalks, cleaned and chopped
1 onion, chopped
4 cloves garlic, minced
1 jalapeño pepper, stemmed, seeded, and chopped
½ cup chopped fresh parsley leaves
3 sprigs fresh thyme
Salt and pepper

FOR SERVING
12 warm flour tortillas
2 cups Refried Beans (page 204)
Onions and Cilantro (page 169)

Rub the meat with the garlic powder and pepper. Light about 25 charcoal briquettes in a chimney and prepare a grill with the coals on one side only. Brown the meat over the hot fire for 10 to 15 minutes, turning often, until well browned. Move it to the cool side of the grill or to the smoking chamber of an offset barbecue smoker. Put some hardwood chips or chunks on the coals and close the lid. Allow the roast to smoke for 1½ to 2 hours at around 250°F, turning to cook evenly.

Meanwhile, in a saucepan over low heat, simmer the tomatillos in water to cover, then turn off the heat. Allow them to sit in the hot water for 5 minutes or until soft. Put the tomatillos in a blender and puree until smooth.

In a soup pot, heat the oil over medium heat and add the celery and onion. Stir and cook for 5 minutes or until softened. Add the garlic and cook another few minutes. Add the tomatillo puree and cook for 3 minutes, stirring well. Add the jalapeño and herbs and 2 cups of water and bring the mixture to a boil.

MAKE SMOKE-BRAISED leg of goat with a big meaty leg from a full-grown goat, not a little *cabrito* leg

Turn down the heat and allow to simmer while the lamb smokes. Season to taste with salt and pepper.

Add more charcoal and wood to the fire. Place a metal roasting pan on the grill directly over the coals. Carefully pour the tomatillo mixture into the roasting pan. Place the meat in the roasting pan with the liquid. Allow the meat to simmer and smoke for 1 hour, turning several times and replenishing the liquid level with water if needed.

With the aid of fire gloves or pot holders, remove the pan from the fire and cover the roast and the roasting pan with aluminum foil and seal tightly. Return to the fire. Simmer over the coals or in a 300°F oven for another hour or two until the meat is extremely tender. You want the shape to be intact, but the meat to be very soft.

Remove the meat from the sauce and allow to cool slightly. Reserve the sauce. Clean the meat away from the bones and chop lightly. Serve the cleaned meat in the green sauce with sauce on the side. Place the tortillas, warm Refried Beans, and Onions and Cilantro on the table. Allow your guests to make their own tacos.

Tex-Mex Asado de Puerco

MAKES ABOUT 2½ POUNDS OF MEAT

BECAUSE OF THE LONG COOKING TIME INVOLVED, I'VE MOVED the final braising step to the oven in this recipe. But if you're a die-hard purist you can do the braising on the grill. Just don't be in a hurry. Like southern pulled pork, this pork isn't done until it turns to mush with the slightest touch.

4-pound pork butt roast
2 tablespoons Tejano Pork Rub (page 21)
3 ancho chiles, seeded and stemmed
5 pitted prunes
½ teaspoon ground cumin
½ teaspoon ground oregano
½ teaspoon ground coriander
½ teaspoon ground cardamom
½ teaspoon ground cinnamon
Dash of ground cloves
2 tablespoons cooking oil
1 onion, minced
4 cloves garlic
3 tablespoons cider vinegar
3 tablespoons honey
1 cup crushed pineapple
4 bay leaves
1 teaspoon salt, or to taste
½ teaspoon freshly ground black pepper
1 tablespoon bittersweet chocolate, cut into small pieces
2 teaspoons grated orange zest
2 cups Refried Beans (page 204)
Warm flour tortillas
Chile Grilled Pineapple (page 208)

Light about 25 charcoal briquettes in a chimney and prepare a grill with the coals on one side only. Season the meat with the pork rub. Sear the meat on all sides over the hot coals and then place in a cooler spot on the grill. Add some wood chips or chunks to the fire and refuel as needed to smoke the pork for 3 or 4 hours. The longer you smoke the pork roast, the less time you will need to braise it.

Meanwhile, roast the chiles on an ungreased skillet over medium heat for 20 to 30 seconds on both sides or until they are aromatic. Place the chiles in a blender with the prunes. Add 3 cups of boiling water, and allow the chiles and prunes to soak until very soft, about 20 minutes. Pour off half of the soaking water and reserve. Add the cumin, oregano, coriander, cardamom, cinnamon, and cloves, and puree. Add back the soaking liquid and blend a few more seconds to mix thoroughly.

Heat a Dutch oven over medium-high heat, then add 2 tablespoons of the oil and the onion and garlic. Cook until the onion is golden brown, but do not allow it to burn. Add the contents of the blender and bring it to a simmer. Add the vinegar, honey, pineapple, bay leaves, and salt and pepper.

After the pork has smoked, bring it inside and preheat the oven to 325°F. Heat the sauce in the Dutch oven on the stovetop while the oven is heating. Place the smoked meat in the Dutch oven with the warm sauce and turn to coat on all sides. Cover and place in the oven and simmer in the sauce, turning the roast every 30 minutes. Continue cooking, adding liquid as needed, until the pork reaches an internal temperature of 185°F or the meat is falling apart. (This step can also be done on the grill, but it will take a lot longer.)

Remove the meat from the pot and set aside. Discard the bay leaves. Skim the grease off and reserve. Reduce the sauce over a burner until it is thick as a milkshake. Stir in the chocolate and orange zest.

Chop and clean the meat. Finely chop the fat that you remove from the roast and use it to make the refried beans.

To serve, arrange the meat on a platter with sauce over the top. Put more sauce in a bowl on the table. Serve the pork with the Refried Beans, tortillas, and grilled pineapple.

NOTE: The flavorful reserved orange-colored grease is called "venom" in Monterrey. Use it to make the refried beans or serve in a crater on top of a bowl of refried beans, a preparation called *frijoles con venoma*.

#6

TAILGATERS ARE known for their creative grilling techniques and bold fashion statements

CHAPTER 6

TEXAS TAILGATING AND WILD GAME

ONA SUNNY SUNDAY AFTERNOON IN NOVEMBER, IN THE parking lot of Reliant Stadium, a few hours before the Houston Texans game, I came upon a city of grills. • I had heard that there was some serious tailgating before the Houston Texans games, so I thought I'd look around the parking lots and get an overview of what people were grilling. But I had no idea what I was getting into. I wrote down recipes until my fingers hurt. And I never even made it past the main gate area.

In front of the main gate, I climbed on top of the school bus with an observation deck to get a look around. From that vantage point, I saw thousands of smoky fires in all directions. There were more plumes of smoke coming from remote parking lots that were more than a mile away.

Houston Texans officials estimate thirty thousand people tailgate before the average home game. In a survey, 52 percent of Texans fans said they ate in the parking lot before the game. When the Texans play Monday Night Football at home, the crowd swells and the cooking gets even more serious. That's when the turduckens and the whole hogs show up.

Why do they do it? What's the point of tailgating? To create fan camaraderie and support the football team, rabid tailgaters will tell you. But these motives hardly explain what tailgating in Texas has become.

It's a party and a pep rally, for sure. But tailgating has become a sport unto itself. These gatherings have turned into the purest form of culinary competitions; this is where the best grillers in Texas go to show off in public. In this small "city" of thirty thousand, there are all kinds of cooks. But nearly all of them are putting on a show.

TAILGATING IN Texas is a tribal bonding ritual

A white-haired gentleman named Sal Ramirez was sitting behind his vehicle grilling on a tiny charcoal grill. He was only cooking a couple of boneless, skinless chicken breasts for himself and a lady friend. But his grapefruit marinade was unique (see the recipe on page 121). And he was quick to point out that the red grapefruits came from his own backyard.

THIS TAILGATER has his jalapeño links custom-made at the Chappel Hill Meat Market by legendary sausage-maker Mike Kopycinski

Nearby, Jacob Trevino flipped his special-recipe stuffed hamburgers. The half-pound patties were made of ground chuck mixed with chopped black olives, chipotle peppers, several kinds of cheese, and Lipton onion soup mix, he told me. Inside each patty, he had created a pocket and stuffed it with cheddar and chiles. (See my version on page 181.) Trevino hunted me down a few hours later so I could try one of his Tex-Mex stuffed burgers. (It was terrific.) Another tailgater, named Gabe Gonzales, handed me a roasted jalapeño stuffed with cream cheese. Most tailgaters bring a little extra food to give away. Some bring a lot of extra food to give away.

Wild game is especially popular at football games. I have seen elk, wild boar, and venison served at tailgate parties. Wild game is great for impressing fellow tailgaters, since you can't buy it at the grocery store or order it in restaurants. Besides, I suspect that in many households, Mom is eager for Dad to get that deer meat out of the freezer. (That's the way it was when I was growing up, anyway.)

In the south parking lot in front of the stadium's main gate, the Raging Bull Tailgaters, winners of the Tailgater of the Year award (which is paid in grocery store coupons) a few years ago, served free food to hundreds of people they had never met before. Each week the team of eight spends two thousand dollars on food. Typically the menu includes half a dozen briskets, half a dozen pork loins, 10 racks of ribs, 30 pounds of chicken wings, 100 pounds of sausage, 40 pounds of shrimp, 20 pounds of fish steaks, and 100 pounds of smoked boudin. There are seldom any leftovers.

Saint Arnold's, the local microbrewery, shows up every week with lots of beer. Stadium rules prohibit charging any money, so everything is free.

Years ago, there was a similar spirit at Texas barbecue cook-offs. But the rigid rules and rising costs ruined all that. Today, barbecue cook-off teams at the Houston Livestock Show and Rodeo Barbecue Cook-off (which is also held in the same parking lot) are required to carry million-dollar liability insurance policies. Successful teams seek corporate sponsorships to defray the expenses. In exchange, the team serves as a caterer for the corporation's functions. You have to have a corporate

OKTOBERFEST CELEBRATION at the football stadium

wristband to get into the party and the barbecuing that was once a joy turns into a job.

Tailgaters grill whatever they want—just for the fun of it. Some put on a big show and some cook quietly with class.

FeedYard Saloon, voted Tailgater of the Year a few years ago, serves brisket and beans to the public from a modern chuck wagon. Family Feud comes in a school bus painted half maroon and half burnt orange—the colors of archrivals Texas A&M and the University of Texas. They serve gourmet tailgating fare including chorizo-stuffed quail and grilled chicken in cilantro cream sauce. The owners of a Mexican-American meat company gave me a taste of a wild boar cooked in a caja china—a Cuban pig-roasting box with a mesquite grill on top. (See La Caja China, page 120.)

Next to grills on trailers the size of my car, I ate medallions of venison backstrap served on hot biscuits with gravy, cheese-stuffed jalapeños wrapped in venison sausage, and grilled shrimp and pineapple kebabs. But I also learned a lot from people sitting in lawn chairs beside tiny propane grills where they cooked grilled asparagus, grilled artichokes, and countless delicacies wrapped in bacon. Bacon is the butcher's string, cooking oil, and garnish, all in one.

Tailgaters are incredibly ingenious. They can bake or steam on the grill with a little aluminum foil. Margarita mix straight out of the bottle becomes an easy marinade for pork, and Bloody Mary mix doubles as a great shrimp cocktail sauce (see the recipe on page 119).

The secret to tailgate grilling is lots of advance preparation. Tailgaters tinker with the seasonings and precook things at home in the kitchen so that when they get to the stadium, there's nothing left to do but throw it on the grill. It's a great technique for backyard grillers, too. Take it from the tailgaters: when you're entertaining in your backyard, do the prep work a day in advance. Then on the day of the party, relax and enjoy.

HOUSTON TEXANS

The Houston Oilers prohibited tailgating at the Astrodome. But when the Texans brought NFL football back to Houston, the new owners decided to promote tailgating as a way to build fan loyalty. The team started the Tailgater of the Game and Tailgater of the Year, competitions that are sponsored by Texas supermarket chain H-E-B. The winner receives a few gift certificates. (Which is next to nothing compared with the huge cash prizes at top barbecue cook-offs.)

Joe Cahn, the self-proclaimed "Commissioner of Tailgating" travels around the country checking out the action. Cahn proclaimed Houston's Reliant Stadium tops in the NFL tailgating scene because of the enormous expanse of the parking lots and the quality of the cooking.

Ancho–Root Beer Hot Wings

MAKES 2 DOZEN

NOW THAT THERE ARE SEVERAL RESTAURANT CHAINS DE-voted to chicken wings, the time when Buffalo hot wings were an ob-scure bar snack found primarily in upstate New York seems like part of ancient history.

24 chicken wings
2 tablespoons Red Rub (page 24)
4 tablespoons (½ stick) butter
1 cup Ancho–Root Beer BBQ sauce (page 27)
1 teaspoon habanero pepper sauce, or to taste
Tex-Mex Ranch Dressing (page 199)
6 celery stalks, cleaned and chopped into short pieces

Set the grill on medium-high heat. Rinse the wings and sprinkle with the rub. Grill the wings, turning often and moving them around to cook evenly. When the wings are well cooked, prepare the wing sauce.

In a flat metal baking pan set on the grill, melt the butter and add the barbe-cue sauce and habanero pepper sauce. When the wings are nicely brown, put them in the pan, shaking and turning to coat with the sauce. Reduce the heat to low. If you have a wing rack, hang the wings from the rack. If you don't have a rack, place the metal pan on the grill or in a medium oven. Cook for 5 to 10 min-utes, turning so that the wing sauce becomes sticky and adheres to the chicken wings. Serve immediately with the dressing and celery stalks.

GRILLING SEASON

In Texas, the grilling seasons are reversed. When most of the country is putting away the Weber for the winter, Texans are tailgating at football games and grilling wild game. The backyard barbecue season is a lot longer in Texas and in most of the South too. Late fall, winter, and early spring are generally the nicest times of the year to eat outside. When south-erners grill in the summer, it's often to avoid heating up the house.

Virgin Mary Grilled Shrimp Cócteles

SERVES 4

TAILGATERS ARE GREAT AT COMING UP WITH NEW USES FOR the ingredients on hand. But this tailgaters' recipe for grilled shrimp cocktails using Bloody Mary mix is sheer genius. The spicy tomato juice makes a much better shrimp cocktail sauce than the ketchup-based glop you get in a lot of restaurants.

Four 8-inch wooden skewers, soaked in water for 15 minutes
1 pound jumbo shrimp (16 shrimp)
½ cup grapefruit juice
¼ cup jalapeño jelly
2 cloves garlic, minced
1 tablespoon vegetable oil
2 tablespoons soy sauce
Cooking spray
2 ripe avocados, sliced
1 cup chopped red onion
Juice of 1 lime
Tabasco sauce, to taste
Bloody Mary Mix (page 49)
½ cup chopped fresh cilantro leaves, for garnish

Thread the shrimp on the soaked wooden skewers. In a measuring cup or small bowl, combine the grapefruit juice, pepper jelly, garlic, oil, and soy sauce. In a baking dish, cover the shrimp with the marinade, cover with plastic wrap, and place in the refrigerator for 30 minutes.

Light the grill. Shake the shrimp skewers to remove excess marinade. Coat the shrimp with cooking spray and grill for 2 to 3 minutes on each side, or until the shrimp are cooked through. Remove from the grill. Remove the shrimp from the skewers.

Divide the avocado slices among 4 martini glasses (or four clear plastic glasses if you're tailgating). Sprinkle with red onion, lime juice, and hot sauce. Add 4 shrimp to each glass. Fill the glass with Bloody Mary Mix (without alcohol) until it just covers the bottom of the shrimp. Garnish with cilantro. Serve with a spoon and saltine crackers or tortilla chips.

THIS CAJA china has a large removable grill with four stout handles. In the cooking chamber below, several pork roasts were being slow-roasted.

LA CAJA CHINA: THE CUBAN PIG ROASTER

The portable pig-roasting box, or caja china, probably originated in Cuba. Beachside food vendors use them to prepare picnic sandwiches in Puerto Rico. The box started turning up on the East Coast a few years ago when a company in Miami started marketing them under the name "La Caja China." The medium-size box sold at the company's website for around three hundred dollars and cooked a seventy-pound whole pig in four hours. The pig comes out with a nice crispy skin, too.

While checking out the tailgating action at Reliant Stadium during football season, I stopped to admire what looked like a charcoal grill loaded with fajita meat and tortillas. But Mariano Moreno, the grill chef, threw me a curve ball. The grill had

a pair of what looked like wheelbarrow handles sticking out of each side. Mariano summoned a friend over and they used these handles to lift up the entire firebox and grill assembly to show me what was below.

In an insulated box underneath the coals, there was a slow-cooking chamber that was big enough to accommodate a whole pig. As it happened, Moreno and company had already cooked and consumed a whole wild hog earlier in the day. Now they were cooking whole sections of beef short ribs in their amazing "Chinese box."

Moreno and company told me they bought their caja china in Monterrey, where the device is often used to slow-roast cabrito.

Grapefruit Chicken Fajitas

SERVES 6

SAL RAMIREZ SAT BEHIND HIS PICK-UP TRUCK GRILLING chicken. He had marinated two boneless, skinless chicken breasts in red grapefruit juice and seasoned them with paprika and lemon pepper.

"You baste the chicken with more grapefruit juice while it's on the grill," he said as he demonstrated his technique. There were more grapefruit sections ready to garnish the finished chicken, which he served in slices over salad greens. "The grapefruit comes from a tree in my backyard," Ramirez told me. He looked to be in his late sixties or early seventies, and he said he used the skinless chicken because he was watching his cholesterol.

Four 7-ounce boneless, skinless chicken breasts
1 clove garlic, minced
2 tablespoons ground Mexican oregano
Juice of 2 Texas red grapefruits
1 tablespoon olive oil
Salt and pepper
6 flour tortillas
Texas Red Grapefruit Salsa (page 222)

Pound the chicken breasts flat between two sheets of plastic wrap. Combine the garlic, Mexican oregano, juice from 1 grapefruit, and olive oil in a mixing bowl. Add the chicken breasts to the mixture and marinate in the refrigerator for at least 4 hours or overnight. Discard the marinade.

Heat the grill. Season the breasts with salt and pepper and grill over hot coals for 2 minutes on each side. Move the chicken to a cooler part of the grill. Cook for 6 to 8 minutes, basting with the juice from the second grapefruit, until cooked through. Heat the tortillas on the grill, turning often. Transfer the chicken breasts to a cutting board and slice them into long strips. Place the chicken strips on a serving platter. Bring to the table (or tailgate) with the warm tortillas, grapefruit salsa, and other condiments such as chopped lettuce or black olives. Invite your guests to make their own fajita tacos.

THE KING OF TEX-MEX: MATT MARTINEZ

Matt Martinez Jr., the King of Tex-Mex, loved to tell stories about his days of playing hooky from school and going fishing and hunting in the wilderness that was once South Austin.

"I spent so much time hunting and fishing, I flunked third grade," he used to say. "The best fishing hole in the city used to be right where Barton Creek emptied into Town Lake," he remembered. "I used to come home with twenty or thirty perch from that spot. You can't even eat the fish from Town Lake anymore."

Matt was a fourth-generation Tex-Mex cook. His grandfather Delphino sold tamales and pecan pralines from a cart he pushed on Congress Avenue before opening El Original, one of the first Tex-Mex restaurants in Austin, in 1925. Matt Senior founded Matt's El Rancho, Austin's quintessential Tex-Mex restaurant, in 1952. Of course, nobody called it Tex-Mex back in those days. In fact, the sign outside of the current location of Matt's El Rancho still boasts THE KING OF MEXICAN FOOD. The term "Tex-Mex" triggers a debate in this family.

Matt Jr.'s sister Gloria Reyna, co-owner of Matt's El Rancho, hates the term. "My grandmother was born in San Luis Potosí. She never called her food Tex-Mex and neither would my Dad," Gloria told me. But Matt was proud and stubborn.

When Englishwoman Diana Kennedy told him that Tex-Mex wasn't real Mexican food, he was insulted. His family came from Mexico and had been cooking in Texas for three generations. But Matt defiantly decided that thenceforward, he would call all his cooking Tex-Mex. And he would help to make Tex-Mex one of the world's most popular cuisines.

He was a great sportsman and wrote regularly for hunting and fishing magazines—mainly about

MATT MARTINEZ JR. demonstrating one of his favorite venison recipes

how to cook wild game. He got his recipe for birds and fish from his grandmother: salt and pepper it, dust it with flour, and pan-fry it in a little *manteca* (lard).

Matt died a few weeks after I interviewed him at his restaurant in Dallas in the spring of 2009. He will be missed by everyone who loves Tex-Mex.

Grilled Backstrap with Peach Glaze

SERVES 4 TO 6, DEPENDING ON THE SIZE OF THE BACKSTRAP

THE BACKSTRAP IS THE TENDERLOIN OF THE VENSION. IT DE-serves to be grilled rare like any good cut of meat. Serve with baked sweet potatoes topped with Chile Butter (page 22).

1 whole venison backstrap
3 tablespoons Tex-Mex Grill Blend (page 21)
¼ cup white wine
2 cups peach preserves
2 tablespoons olive oil

Prepare the grill. Remove any silver skin from the backstrap. Cut the meat across the grain into thick serving pieces (about 2 inches each). Sprinkle the seasoning blend on the meat, turning to season both sides. In a saucepan, heat the white wine to boiling and cook until reduced by half. Blend in the preserves and cook over medium heat until liquefied. Set aside.

Brush a little olive oil on each piece of meat and place the meat on the grill. Cook for about 4 minutes. Turn and cook for another 3 minutes, then brush with the glaze. When the meat is done to your liking, turn it one more time and brush the other side with the glaze. Cook until the glaze just begins to bubble. (The glaze has to be added at the last minute or it will burn.) Serve immediately.

Venison Sausage

MAKES 12 POUNDS

VARIATIONS

For wild boar sausage, substitute wild boar or feral hog meat for the venison. For spicy hot, substitute a bottle of pickled jalapeños and their juice for the pickle juice and add ¼ cup or more of salt.

MAKING LINK SAUSAGE IS COMPLICATED, BUT MAKING PATTY sausage is fairly simple. And there's lots of things to do with it besides cooking it for breakfast; try making Grilled Stuffed Peppers (page 131) and Atomic Deer Turds (page 128).

5 pounds fatty pork butt
5 pounds venison shoulder, cut into pieces
2 pounds salt pork, rind removed
½ cup coarsely ground black pepper
2 cups pickle juice
10 whole cloves garlic
1 teaspoon oil for frying

Grind the pork butt, venison, and salt pork together through a ¼-inch plate of a meat grinder. Add the pepper, pickle juice, and garlic cloves a little at a time in the top of the grinder along with the pieces of meat so that the spices become well incorporated in the meat. In a large bowl, knead the mixture with your hands until everything is well blended.

In a small skillet, heat the oil. Form a portion of the mixture into a small patty and fry. Taste for seasonings, and adjust to your taste. At this point you can divide the sausage into 1-pound packages and freeze for patty sausage.

Armadillo Eggs

MAKES 4

THE INITIAL BURN OF THE JALAPEÑO IS PRETTY INTENSE, BUT it quickly subsides into a pleasant mouth buzz that goes great with cold beer. The main trick to taming the heat is to clean out all the white inner membrane and seeds from the jalapeño. Other methods of cooling it down include starting with grilled jalapeños or cutting the pepper into smaller chunks.

4 small jalapeño peppers
Four 1-inch chunks of cheese
4 strips bacon

Cut the tops off the jalapeños. Hollow out the inside of the bottom end of the pepper, removing all of the seeds and as much of the white pith as possible without puncturing the chile. Cut some cheese so that it fits inside the pepper. Wrap with bacon and secure with a toothpick pushed through the middle of the pepper.

Light the grill. Cook the peppers over medium heat, turning often, for about 15 minutes or until the bacon is well browned. Serve immediately.

MATT MARTINEZ'S BACON WRAPPING TRICK

"Stuff it with a jalapeño and wrap it with bacon" is pretty much the standard hunting-camp recipe for anything. Matt Martinez Jr. showed me a neat trick for bacon wrapping. He pounded the bacon with the side of a meat cleaver to make it thinner and more elastic. It sticks to the meat better and cooks faster, too.

LEGENDARY BAR-
BECUE man Rick
Schmidt grills some
dove and quail
poppers on the pit
at Kreuz Market in
Lockhart

Rick Schmidt's Bird Poppers

MAKES 12

RICK SCHMIDT OF KREUZ MARKET IN Lockhart, the most famous barbecue joint in Texas, told me to call him up a day in advance and he'd put some quail on for lunch sometime. I called and he made good on his promise.

He cooked up a couple dozen quail and about a dozen doves on the smoker at Kreuz Market. Each had a small round of pepper neatly tucked into a slit on the side of the bird instead of the usual half a pepper stuck in the breast cavity. He cooked the "running gear," as he called the legs, separately on a piece of aluminum foil.

"With birds it's best to start out cooking them slow and then finish them on a hot fire," Rick said as he took them off the pit.

1 tablespoon pepper jelly or peach preserves
¼ cup white wine
12 jalapeño pepper slices or 6 peppers, halved and seeded
12 whole dove breasts or whole quail breasts
12 strips bacon
12 toothpicks
Salt and pepper

Light the grill. Combine the jelly and wine in a small pan on the grill. Place a pepper slice into a slit in each dove or quail breast, wrap with bacon, and secure with a toothpick. Or place a pepper half inside the breastbone of each bird and wrap with a strip of bacon and secure with a toothpick. Place the poppers on the slow part of the grill and cook slowly for 15 or 20 minutes, until the meat is rosy inside; then paint with the glaze and move to the hot part of the grill until the bacon is crispy, about 5 more minutes. Season with salt and pepper and serve.

Atomic Deer Turds

MAKES 4 HALVES

INSTEAD OF BACON (SEE Armadillo Eggs, PAGE 125), SOME tailgaters prefer to wrap their stuffed jalapeños with breakfast sausage. I also saw a tailgating team using butterflied venison backstrap medallions as the outer layer—but the very best meat for this use is venison sausage.

    2 small jalapeño peppers
    Two 1-inch chunks of cheese
    6 to 8 ounces cold Venison Sausage (page 124; or substitute pork sausage
        or ground beef)
    Cooking spray

Cut the tops off the jalapeños. Hollow out the inside of the bottom end of the pepper, removing all of the seeds and as much of the white pith as possible without puncturing the chile. Cut some cheese so that it fits inside the pepper. Flatten a cold 3- to 4-ounce patty of Venison Sausage on a cutting board with your palm. Peel it up and fold it around the stuffed pepper, squeezing to form an oblong shape and sealing the pepper inside. The sausage-wrapped peppers can be made in advance to this point and stored in the refrigerator for several days.

Light the grill. Spray some oil in a skillet or griddle and cook the stuffed sausage over medium heat, turning often, for about 15 minutes or until well browned on all sides. Allow to cool enough to handle, then, with a sharp knife, cut each oblong in half so you can see the pepper and cheese. Serve immediately.

Grilled Quail with Cilantro Cream

SERVES 6

IT'S NOT EASY TO BONE OUT A QUAIL AND LEAVE THE MEAT IN one piece. That's why most hunters grill game birds with the breast meat still on the bone as in the recipe for poppers on page 127. But when you buy quail at the store, they come neatly cleaned. That's when you want to try a fancier presentation like this. There isn't a lot of meat on a quail, so don't count on serving them as a main dish at dinner, but they make a delicious addition to a mixed grill.

> 6 quail, boneless
> 1 teaspoon olive oil
> 2 tablespoons Red Rub (page 24)
> 3 tablespoons honey, warm
> Cilantro Cream (page 201)

Rinse the quail and rub with the oil, then sprinkle with Red Rub and allow to marinate in the refrigerator for 30 minutes.

Light the grill. Place the quail on the slow part of the grill and cook slowly for 15 or 20 minutes, turning once, until the meat is rosy inside; then paint with the honey and move to the hot part of the grill, turning frequently, until the glaze bubbles, about 5 more minutes. Remove from the grill. Drizzle the quail with Cilantro Cream and serve immediately as part of a mixed grill or as an appetizer.

SEASON THE meat extra spicy and don't overfill the bell-pepper halves when you make Grilled Stuffed Peppers

Grilled Stuffed Peppers

MAKES 6 SMALL STUFFED PEPPER HALVES

STUFFED PEPPERS COME OUT WELL ON THE GRILL IF YOU DON'T make them too big. I like to mix ground meats and season the stuffed peppers heavily. Be sure to cook a little of the meat mixture to test the seasonings before you stuff the peppers, since the salt and spice levels of the various sausage meats and seasoning mixes vary widely.

2 tablespoons seasoning blend of your choice
1 teaspoon salt (omit if there is salt in the seasoning mix)
½ cup white wine
½ pound Venison Sausage (page 124; or substitute breakfast
   sausage meat)
½ pound ground beef
1 cup cooked rice
2 cloves garlic, minced
1 egg, beaten
½ cup minced fresh parsley leaves
Cayenne pepper
Ground cumin
Oil, for frying
3 small green bell peppers (four lobes preferred)

VARIATIONS
LEB-MEX PEPPERS
Use kebab seasoning such as Sadaf, available in Middle Eastern grocery stores.

CAJUN PEPPERS
Use a Cajun spice blend such as Tony Chachere's or Zatarain's and omit the salt.

Mix the seasoning blend, salt, and wine in a small bowl and stir well. Then combine the mixture with all the other ingredients except the oil and peppers in a mixing bowl and mash with your hands until all the ingredients are evenly distributed. Put the meat in the refrigerator for an hour or more to allow the flavors to blend.

Heat a little oil in a frying pan and place a teaspoon of the meat mixture in the hot oil. Cook, turning frequently, until done on both sides. Taste, and adjust the salt and seasonings in the remaining meat mixture.

Cut the peppers in half through the stem so that they form six half-pepper cups. Fill each half pepper with meat mixture. Mound the meat no more than a ½ inch over the top edge of each pepper. The stuffed peppers can be made in advance to this point and stored covered in the refrigerator for several days.

Light the grill. Cook pepper side down over low heat for 10 to 12 minutes, until the pepper is charred and soft. Turn the stuffed peppers over and cook on the meat side for 10 minutes. Test for doneness. Serve immediately with your choice of salsas. These are also great cold or cut into slices for sandwiches.

#7

A SHRIMP STALL at an open-air seafood market on the Mexican Gulf Coast

CHAPTER 7

BIG FISH AND BROWN SHRIMP

THE SHRIMP FAJITAS AT THE PALMETTO INN ON SOUTH Padre Island come in a sizzling comal with onions and peppers. They are made with fresh Texas brown shrimp. The chain originated in Brownsville, home of the state's largest shrimp fleet. • "We started serving seafood in 1962 at the Palmetto Inn's Shrimp Boat restaurant in Brownsville," Christy Carrasco, the restaurant's owner, told me. Though I had eaten at the Palmetto Inn on beach vacations on South Padre Island before, I was clueless about the chain's long history until I met Christy and started asking questions.

She invited me to meet her at the restaurant one afternoon. I found her waiting with a big brown envelope full of old photos. The first Palmetto Inn was opened in Brownsville in 1945 by Christy's father-in-law, Moises M. Carrasco, she said. She showed me photos of the Palmetto's founding father. He looked like he knew how to enjoy himself. There were photos of Moises and the family on a sailboat in Acapulco and several photos of trophy sailfish they had landed on deep-sea fishing expeditions.

Moises had six children and as the family grew, his heirs built restaurants in high-traffic locations in Harlingen, McAllen, Corpus Christi, Weslaco, and San Antonio. The northernmost location of Palmetto Inn was on "The Circle" in Waco across from the legendary Elite Circle Grill.

Not only did Moises Carrasco serve fresh shrimp at his restaurants, he also signed a license with Colonel Sanders for Palmetto Inns to become the first outlets for the Colonel's famous fried chicken—long before the Kentucky Fried Chicken chain had its own locations.

She showed me pictures of what the Palmetto Inns had once looked like. I loved the old cars and the neon signs. I particularly liked a photo of Nancy Reagan eating dinner with Roger Staubach with a gaudy velvet painting on the wall behind them.

The Palmetto Inn chain not only introduced Tex-Mex seafood and the Colonel's fried chicken to South Texans, it became one of the most successful restaurant chains in the state. The end came suddenly when the interstate highway system debuted in the early 1960s. The limited-access freeways diverted traffic from the cross-country routes and doomed the old-fashioned roadhouse restaurants that once thrived all across Texas.

"When I-35 was completed, Moises started closing the restaurants," Christy said. "It was just like what happened to those wonderful diners along Route 66."

The Palmetto Inn location in McAllen was recently sold to one of its employees, who renamed it Garcia's. The South Padre Island location is the last remnant of the once proud chain and serves as a reminder of where Tex-Mex seafood dishes like shrimp fajitas got started.

"This is all that's left," Christy said, pointing to the walls of the old hurricane-battered building around her. "It's the end of an era."

A SIZZLING COMAL
of shrimp fajitas at
the Palmetto Inn on
South Padre Island

Wild Texas Brown Shrimp

TEXAS REMAINS ONE OF AMERICA'S top shrimp-producing states, but the fishery is in decline. Wild Gulf Coast brown shrimp are being replaced in the marketplace by imported farm-raised white shrimp. Outside of Texas, consumers like the milder flavor of white shrimp better.

Gulf brown shrimp have a distinctive aroma and taste that most consumers describe as an "iodine flavor." The chemical is actually bromine, not iodine, according to Russell Miget, associate professor of seafood technology for Texas A&M University. The "iodine flavor" has no relationship to the dark vein on the back of the shrimp. That vein, which is actually the digestive tract, does not affect flavor. There is no reason for its removal other than aesthetics (or squeamishness).

About half of the shrimp sold in Texas is brown shrimp and it's one of the only places where it's still eaten, according to Jim Gossen of Louisiana Foods, one of the largest shrimp dealers in Houston. That bromine or iodine flavor comes from the kelp that brown shrimp in the Gulf of Mexico feed on.

White shrimp is the only kind of shrimp that's farm-raised and it's become the dominant shrimp sold in the United States, Gossen said. Whether they are white or brown, wild shrimp have a richer flavor and firmer texture than farm-raised shrimp because they feed on crustaceans and seaweed and swim freely.

Limited amounts of pink shrimp and various imported species like Thai tiger shrimp are available in Texas, too. Tiger shrimp are mild-tasting shrimp that are predominantly farm-raised in Asia. These shrimp are not as dense as the white or brown gulf shrimp. They are lower in cost, have a higher moisture content, and shrink more when cooked.

"When you are cooking spicy food, you need to have a stronger shrimp flavor. That's when I would use brown shrimp," Gossen told me. "I like to use white shrimp for delicate dishes like shrimp scampi."

TWO GIANT dueling shrimp with cowboy hats and six-shooters once graced the parking lot of Christie's Seafood Restaurant on South Main in Houston

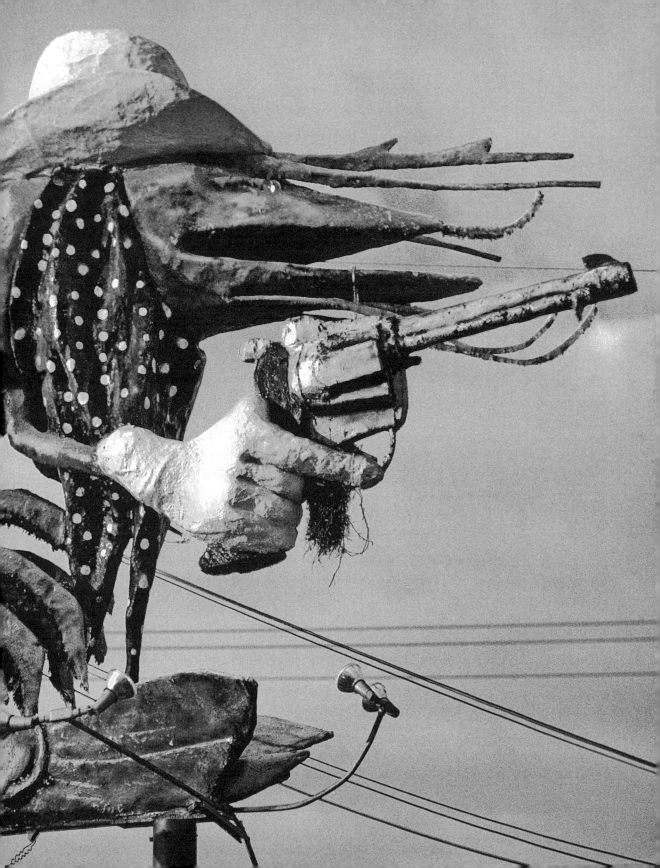

Palmetto Inn Shrimp Fajitas

SERVES 2

AT THE PALMETTO INN, THE SHRIMP, ONIONS, AND GREEN PEP-
pers are brought to the table on a sizzling comal with warm flour tortillas, lime
wedges, guacamole, and cold beer. You can serve them with shredded lettuce
and chopped tomatoes if you prefer—just don't forget the guacamole.

1 pound large shrimp, shelled
1 tablespoon vegetable oil
1 clove garlic, minced
1 teaspoon ground Mexican oregano
Sea salt and freshly ground black pepper
Cooking spray
1 onion, sliced
1 green bell pepper, coarsely chopped
1 lime
6 warm flour tortillas
Lime wedges
All-American Guacamole, chilled (page 197)

In a mixing bowl, toss the shrimp with the oil, garlic, oregano, salt, and pepper
and allow to marinate for 30 minutes in the refrigerator.

Using the medium setting on a gas grill or a low charcoal fire, heat up a
griddle or comal that fits on the grill. You will need a lid that will fit over the
shrimp as it cooks. Oil the griddle with some cooking spray and start cooking the onion and bell pepper. Place the cover over the vegetables and allow
the steam to soften them, removing the cover and stirring every few minutes.
When the onion and pepper are nicely browned, add the shrimp and stir. Allow
the shrimp to cook for 2 or 3 minutes, until they begin to turn opaque. Squeeze
the lime juice over the shrimp and cover to capture the steam. The shrimp are
done when they begin to curl, about 5 to 7 minutes total cooking time depending on the heat of the fire and the size of the shrimp. Do not overcook. Remove
the shrimp and vegetables and serve immediately with tortillas, lime wedges,
guacamole, and your favorite beverage.

Grilled Shrimp and Guacamole Salad

SERVES 4

YOU'LL ENJOY THE CONTRAST OF THE HOT SHRIMP AND COLD guacamole in this "hot and cold" salad.

Four 8-inch wooden skewers, soaked in water for 15 minutes
1 pound jumbo shrimp (16 shrimp)
½ cup Texas red grapefruit juice
¼ cup jalapeño jelly
2 cloves garlic, minced
1 tablespoon vegetable oil
2 tablespoons soy sauce
Cooking spray
1 head of butter lettuce, leaves washed, cleaned, and dried
All-American Guacamole, chilled (page 197)
Sea salt
1 Texas red grapefruit, supremed (page 149) and chilled
Cilantro sprigs, for garnish
Green onion shavings, for garnish
4 lime wedges, for garnish

Place the shrimp on the soaked wooden skewers. Combine the grapefruit juice, pepper jelly, garlic, oil, and soy sauce in a small bowl. In a baking dish, cover the shrimp with the marinade; cover with plastic wrap and place in the refrigerator for 30 minutes.

Light the grill. Shake the shrimp skewers to remove excess marinade. Coat the shrimp with cooking spray and grill for about 2 to 3 minutes on each side, or until the shrimp are cooked through. Remove from the grill.

Arrange the lettuce leaves in a bed on 4 chilled salad plates. Divide the guacamole among the plates, placing it in a lettuce "cup" in the center of each plate. Remove the shrimp from the skewers and place 4 shrimp on top of the guacamole and season with salt to taste. Arrange the grapefruit supremes around the shrimp on the bed of lettuce. Garnish with the cilantro, green onion shavings, and lime wedges. Serve immediately.

SHRIMP KEBABS are a favorite tailgating appetizer—the grilled shrimp are also great for shrimp cocktails

John Hamman's Shrimp Kebabs

SERVES 4

JOHN'S TAILGATING TEAM WAS MAKING THESE INCREDIBLY colorful appetizers when I stopped by their huge trailer parked in front of Reliant Stadium in Houston. These guys are actually a race car team that spends most of their time at auto racing events. When the racing season is over, they start slumming with the football fans. But wherever they go, they sure eat well.

16 jumbo shrimp
20 1-inch squares bell pepper
20 1-inch squares red onion
20 1-inch squares pineapple
Four 10-inch wooden skewers, soaked in water for 15 minutes

FOR THE MARINADE
1 cup pineapple juice
¼ cup olive oil
¼ cup Worcestershire sauce
2 tablespoons garlic powder
Sea salt to taste
Freshly ground black pepper to taste

Clean and shell the shrimp. Alternate the bell pepper, onion, pineapple, and shrimp on the skewers. Combine the marinade ingredients in a mixing bowl. Place the skewers in a baking dish, pour the marinade over the top, and turn the skewers to coat well. Grill over medium heat until the shrimp are cooked through and beginning to curl, between 5 and 7 minutes depending on the heat of the fire and the size of the shrimp. Do not overcook.

Garlic Grilled Oysters
MAKES 12

IT WAS DRAGO'S IN METAIRIE, LOUISIANA, THAT MADE CHAR-
broiled oysters famous. Jimmy G's on Sam Houston Parkway in Houston does
a great job with them too. Gilhooley's does them over a pecan wood fire that
gives the oysters a wonderful smoky flavor. Also known as barbecued oysters,
these are made by putting a fresh shucked oyster on a grill and spooning in
some melted butter and garlic; you can add parmesan if you like.

4 tablespoons (½ stick) butter
4 cloves garlic, minced
Salt and freshly ground black pepper
12 freshly shucked oysters
Freshly grated parmesan cheese (optional)

Melt the butter in a pan, add the garlic, and add salt and pepper to taste. Heat a
grill. Put the shucked oysters over the hot part of the fire. When the shell gets
hot, the oysters will quickly begin to sizzle. Divide the garlic butter among the
oysters. Don't be alarmed if the butter causes the fire to flare up; it adds a char-
grilled flavor. Sprinkle parmesan over the top after the butter, if desired. Serve
immediately with crusty bread for dipping.

IT TAKES a while for the shells to heat up—then the oysters flare up as the butter boils over

Dorado BLT Tacos

SERVES 8

DAVID GARRIDO SERVES THESE AT HIS UPSCALE TACO BAR IN Austin. The fish they call mahimahi in Hawaii is called dorado in the Gulf of Mexico. It has a bold flavor that tastes great with hot sauce and bacon, lettuce, and tomato on a taco.

1 pound dorado (mahimahi) fillets
Olive oil
2 tablespoons powdered chile (see page 233)
8 tortillas (see Taquero-Style Tacos, page 164)
4 slices bacon, fried crisp and crumbled
1 cup chopped iceberg lettuce
1 tomato, seeded and diced
½ cup salsa of your choice
1 cup Cilantro Cream (page 201)

Prepare the grill. Coat the fish evenly on both sides with olive oil and chile powder. Place the fish on the grill over medium-high heat and cook for 2 to 3 minutes. Turn and cook for 3 minutes longer, or until just done. Do not overcook or the fish will be tough. Remove from the grill and cut the fish into strips, removing any skin or bones. Divide the fish among the tortillas. Top with the bacon, lettuce, tomato, salsa, and Cilantro Cream.

Big Fish Steaks

SERVES 4 TO 6

IN THE HEYDAY OF THE PALMETTO INN CHAIN, MOISES CAR-
rasco used to take the family to Acapulco every year. Deep-sea fishing was
among Moises's favorite pastimes. In those days, eating the fish was part of
the experience. Today, most trophy-size fish are taken by catch-and-release
fishermen. After a few photographs, which are used to re-create a replica of
the fish for mounting, the swordfish or marlin is thrown back. Of course, you
can find swordfish in the seafood store and some marlin are still eaten in Mexican resorts. Fish steaks from big fish like swordfish, marlin, shark, or tuna are
great cooked on a hot grill and drizzled with a little citrus-pepper sauce. Err on
the rare side; fish steaks get tough quickly if overdone.

**THE CARRASCO family
loved to go deep-sea fishing**

2 pounds fresh swordfish, marlin, shark, or tuna steaks
Salt and freshly ground black pepper
Juice of 2 limes
1 clove garlic, minced
½ serrano or habanero pepper, seeds and stem removed, minced
¼ cup vegetable oil

Season the fish steaks with salt and pepper. Combine the lime juice, garlic,
serrano or habanero pepper, and oil in a bowl and toss the steaks in this mixture. Let marinate for 15 minutes. Grill quickly over a medium-hot grill, about
5 minutes per side for a 1-inch-thick steak, 2½ minutes per side for a ½-inch
steak. Drizzle the marinade over the steaks as they cook. Do not overcook.

WAITRESSES IN costume at the Palmetto Inn in the 1960s

Republic of the Rio Grande Grilled Tuna and Grapefruit Supreme Salad

SERVES 4

A RESTAURANT IN MCALLEN, TEXAS, CALLED REPUBLIC OF THE Rio Grande Grill and Cantina invented this entrée-size grilled tuna salad with grapefruit sections and red onions on top. It's a classic combination of South Texas flavors—and a very healthy dinner.

2 ½ Texas red grapefruits
1 tablespoon white wine vinegar
¾ cup olive oil
1 clove garlic, minced
¼ teaspoon salt
Freshly ground black pepper
1 teaspoon minced jalapeño pepper, or hot pepper sauce
4 tuna steaks, 6 to 8 ounces each
6 cups mixed salad greens
2 tablespoons chopped fresh cilantro leaves
8 red onion slices

Peel and supreme 2 grapefruits (page 149); set aside. Squeeze the juice from the other half grapefruit into a measuring cup; it should yield about ¼ cup of juice.

To make the salad dressing, combine the grapefruit juice, vinegar, oil, garlic, salt, freshly ground black pepper to taste, and minced jalapeño in a medium bowl; mix well. Cover and refrigerate the salad dressing.

Place the tuna steaks in a shallow dish. Pour 1 tablespoon of dressing over each piece of tuna. Turn the tuna in the marinade to coat. Cover with plastic wrap, or place all of the tuna steaks and marinade in a plastic bag, and refrigerate for 1 hour.

Light the grill. Remove the tuna from the refrigerator and allow to come to room temperature. Grill for about 4 minutes per inch of thickness for rare, 6 minutes for medium or until done to taste, turning at least once.

To serve, toss the greens with the salad dressing in a mixing bowl. Divide the dressed greens among 4 plates. Top each with a grilled tuna steak, then sprinkle with freshly ground black pepper. Spread grapefruit supremes over the top of the salad. Garnish with the cilantro and red onion slices.

Grapefruit Supremes

When I was a kid, the thing I liked best about grapefruit was that you got to spoon unlimited amounts of sugar on it. I remember broiled grapefruit with brown sugar on top, too; the sugar caramelized into a crunchy candy coating. Back then, everybody knew that grapefruit was too sour to eat unsweetened, especially for kids. Today, I would never think of pouring sugar on a Texas red grapefruit. And neither would my kids. They like their grapefruit without sugar, thank you, but they still insist that Dad section it out for them into skinless "supremes."

Supremes of grapefruit are a spectacular topping for salads or seafood dishes. They are also called for in the awesome Texas Red Grapefruit Salsa on page 222.

HOW TO SUPREME A GRAPEFRUIT

CUT OFF all the peel, the white pith, and the outer part of the membrane that surrounds each section of grapefruit.

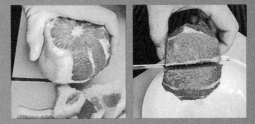

SLIDE A KNIFE in between the fruit and the membrane on one side and "flip" the naked fruit out of the membrane and into a bowl. Repeat with every section. Squeeze the juice from any remaining bits of fruit into the bowl.

Tampico Snapper a la Plancha

SERVES 4

JOHN STAGE IS THE FOUNDER OF DINOSAUR BAR-B-QUE, A FAmous barbecue joint in New York. Stage called me when he was in Houston a couple of years ago. He and his posse had already eaten a lot of Texas barbecue and they wanted some Gulf seafood for a change. So I took them to Tampico, a Mexican *ostioneria* (oyster bar) and grill. We ordered Mexican beers and tequila shots and some shrimp *cócteles*.

For our entrée, I dragged Stage to the fish counter. The beauty of Tampico's Mexican seafood market concept is that the whole fish are kept up front on a bed of ice. You pick out the exact fish you want and pay for it by the pound. There are several varieties depending on the season, but my top choice is Gulf red snapper, which is referred to here by its Mexican name, *huachinango* (pronounced "watch-ee-NONG-o").

When you order whole snapper *a la plancha,* you get the fish griddle-cooked with onions and green peppers. It runs eleven dollars a pound, and a five-pound fish will feed a big crowd. I usually add a pound of shrimp and a couple pairs of frog's legs to turn my huachinango a la plancha into a custom seafood platter.

1 whole red snapper, about 2 pounds
½ cup olive oil
2 onions, one minced and one cut into thick slices
3 tablespoons freshly squeezed lemon juice
1 tablespoon ground Mexican oregano
Cooking spray
1 green bell pepper, cored, seeded, and cut into thick slices
½ pound shrimp, shelled and cleaned

Light the grill. Clean and scale the snapper. Rinse the fish and cut off the gill fins. With a sharp knife, make three vertical slashes about 1½ inches apart along each side of the fish all the way to the bone.

Combine the olive oil, minced onion, lemon juice, and oregano in a small bowl. Put the fish in a large baking dish. Bend the fish so that the slashes open along one side. Spoon the marinade into the fish. Repeat on the other side. Marinate in the refrigerator for 30 minutes.

Spray a griddle or comal with cooking spray and cook the sliced onion and bell pepper over low heat on one side of the grill. Set the other side of the grill to medium heat. Spread the fish apart so it stands on its rib cage and cook the fish standing up on the grill over medium heat for 10 minutes. Put the onion and pepper mixture aside and move the fish to the griddle or comal. Cook the fish on one side for 5 minutes, then turn and cook for 5 minutes on the other side or until cooked through. Total cooking time should be roughly 10 minutes per inch of thickness. Add the shrimp to the griddle or comal during the last 3 minutes of cooking.

To impress the crowd, load a platter or a sizzling comal with the caramelized onions and peppers and place the whole fish on top. (You can also use a platter.) When the fish is cooked through, the flesh will fall away from the bone easily along the slash lines when you carve it. Serve with tortillas and condiments of your choice.

WHOLE FISH

Cooking a whole fish on a grill is a challenge. Fish has a tendency to stick to the grill and fall apart. There are accessories such as fish baskets and fine-mesh grill overlays to make it easier. This is where a comal or griddle comes in handy. You can start the fish on the grill to get some grill marks and color, and then transfer it to the comal to finish it. If you don't have a comal, you can also use aluminum foil. For a really easy method, check out the recipe for Redfish on the Half Shell (page 152).

Redfish on the Half Shell

SERVES 4

HERE IS AN OLD TEXAS FISH-CAMP RECIPE: YOU FILLET THE fish, but leave the scales on. Then grill the fish on the scale side only, basting often. The scales curl up to hold the marinade. When it's done, the fish slides right off the blackened scales, which usually stick to the grill.

2 cloves garlic, minced
2 tablespoons minced fresh flat-leaf parsley leaves
¼ cup olive oil
Juice of 1 lemon, plus 1 lemon cut into wedges
Salt and pepper
One 3- to 4-pound redfish, filleted, scales left on

Light the grill. Place the garlic, parsley, olive oil, and lemon juice into a mixing bowl and whisk well. Lightly salt and pepper the fish fillets. Over a medium fire, place the fish, skin down, on the grill grate. Cook slowly for about 30 minutes, basting with the olive oil and lemon juice mixture every 5 minutes. When the fish is cooked through, pull gently to see if the skin is stuck to the grill. If it is, slide a large spatula carefully between the skin and the meat, removing the meat from the grill while leaving the skin. If the skin isn't stuck to the grill, you can separate the skin from the fillet on the serving platter.

Remove any skin or bones and divide the two fillets into four servings. Moisten with any leftover olive oil and lemon mixture. Serve immediately with lemon wedges.

MESQUITE-GRILLED fish filet on a sizzling platter at Goode Company Seafood in Houston

AN IDYLLIC setting for
a taco-trailer picnic on
South Lamar in Austin

CHAPTER 8

TACO TRUCK TAQUITOS AND TORTABURGERS

THE *BISTEC* TACO AT THE JARRO TRAILER ON GESSNER Drive in West Houston came with Angus sirloin, sliced paper-thin without a thread of gristle, grilled well-done, and layered on two lightly fried corn tortillas. On the stainless-steel counter that runs along the front of the trailer, there were salsas and condiments in six *molcajetes*, the three-legged Mexican bowls typically used as mortars.

I grabbed a fat lime quarter from one bowl on the shelf and squeezed it over the top of the steak. I skipped the bright orange *chile de árbol* salsa and the neon green serrano slurry. This time I wanted to try a dark-chocolate-colored salsa made with dried chiles in oil with a dash of orange juice for sweetness. For a topping, I spooned up some "Mayan escabeche," electric purple onion slices marinated in lime juice, flecked with Mexican oregano and chile powder.

I folded the two tortillas around the meat and condiments, cocked my head to one side in the time-honored taco eater's pose, and took a huge bite. The meat was so tender, it dissolved on my tongue. The juicy beef melded with the familiar flavors of corn tortilla and lime juice. The raw-flavored dried chile salsa came on like mole poblano's punk-ass cousin. And the juicy raw onions added some crunch.

It was one of the most impressive tacos I ate in the six months of writing the "Taco Truck Gourmet" column for the Houston Press food blog. I have eaten a lot of tacos while writing about taco trucks, carnecerias (Mexican meat markets), and taquerias over the past few years.

The trucks are interesting places to eat Mexican food in Hispanic cities like Los Angeles and my hometown of Houston. But in formerly virgin taco territories such as Portland, Seattle, New Orleans, and New York City, taco trucks and the newly opened hole-in-the-wall taquerias are selling the best Mexican food in town.

THE "TACO TRUCK GOURMET" BLOG got started one morning when I tried to get breakfast at the famous taco trailer called Taqueria Tacambaro behind the Farmer's Marketing Association produce terminal on Airline Drive. The proprietress, Maria Rojas, didn't have any egg tacos. She said she only had fajitas. I pointed to a pile of white things on the griddle and asked her what they were.

"Mollejas," she replied, which is Spanish for sweetbreads. The incongruity of eating a dish I associated with French haute cuisine from a taco truck made me grin. Just for kicks, I ordered a taco stuffed with sweetbreads and topped it with raw onion, cilantro, and salsa. The fluffy, barely-cooked-through sweetbreads, hot off the griddle, were the best I have ever eaten in Houston.

Maria Rojas told me that she served the same food at her taco trailer that you would find at the little *puestos* (food stalls) in the *mercado* of her hometown of Tacambaro in Michoacán. She chose her location near the fruit and vegetable stands of the Farmer's

A TACO truck in line for cleaning at the Southwest Commissary in Houston—the health department requires a visit every twenty-four hours

TACO TRUCK HISTORY

The concept of the taco truck isn't as new as it seems. Fresh tortillas, fried tortilla chips, and Mexican snacks were delivered door-to-door by horse and buggy in San Antonio in the 1800s. Tamale carts and other mobile food vendors were also very common in Texas before the sanitary laws of the Progressive Era were enacted in the early 1900s and shut them down.

The first actual taco trucks in Texas were Model T Fords. A 1939 black-and-white photograph (shown above) by the famous WPA photographer Russell Lee captured the details. It's titled "Mexican lunch wagon serving tortillas and fried beans to workers in pecan shelling plant, San Antonio, Texas."

In the photo, the taco vendor squats in the back of a Model T pickup truck with a cardboard box full of tortillas. His customers take the desired number of tortillas and make "self-serve" tacos from a selection of fillings in metal pots arrayed along the edge of the open tailgate. It illustrates a unique solution to the lack of handwashing facilities: *el taquero,* the taco man, never touches the tacos.

Marketing Association because it is the closest thing to a Mexican mercado you can find in Houston.

I might never have tried the taco de mollejas at Taqueria Tacambaro, if they hadn't been the only thing available. The experience convinced me that there were some hidden treasures out there. So I decided to make a concerted effort to find the best taco trucks in the city.

I already knew that there was nothing inherently wonderful about taco truck food. It can be better than, worse than, or just the same as the food in a taqueria or a Mexican restaurant. But there are some fundamental differences.

Taco trucks are operated by immigrants for immigrants. And this makes them a fascinating culinary phenomenon. First of all, because they are serving some items that no other venues offer. And secondly, because they challenge high-minded ideas about authenticity.

Taco-truck fare is defined by the Mexican-style taco, which is comprised of two lightly fried corn tortillas stuck together, and then filled with some kind of meat. The price ranges from a dollar to two dollars each, with the vast majority falling smack in the middle at $1.50.

On Texas taco trucks, you always find barbacoa (beef cheek meat), pork carnitas (little bits of pork), and tacos al pastor (see page 171). Breakfast tacos and hamburguesas are also popular. But by far the most common offering is fajitas—various papain-tenderized cuts of beef that meat purveyors sell very cheap.

The taquero will ask if you want raw onion and chopped cilantro, which is generally free. For the second tier of garnishes, an additional option of lettuce and tomato, there is generally a small charge. Jalapeños, sometimes pickled but more often roasted, are also available for a pittance. Salsas range from the simple to the elaborate; they are always free and are always applied by the consumer.

Variations include other corn dough platforms, such as *gorditas, chalupas,* or *sopes,* which go for two to three dollars. Flour tortillas are sometimes available for an extra twenty-five cents, and they are occasionally homemade. The oversized Mexican sandwiches called *tortas* are priced at five

MARIA ROJAS and her knockout sweetbread tacos at the Farmer's Marketing Association in Houston

to six dollars. I have also seen Frito pie and nachos on taco-truck menus, but Tex-Mex crispy tacos and cheese enchiladas are notably absent.

There are also specialists. *Pollo asado* (roasted chicken) is offered by brightly painted school buses with names like Regio or Norteño that suggest the owners come from Monterrey. The chicken trucks are equipped with mesquite grills and turn out an excellent whole chicken dinner that comes with a roasted onion, peppers, salsas, and tortillas for ten dollars.

Even though the cooks and the customers are mostly Mexican immigrants, it would be a mistake to assume that taco trucks serve authentic Mexican food. Goat is the most common meat in the Michoacán mercado stalls, Maria Rojas told me. I have had taco-truck *birria* (stewed goat) a couple of times, but it's not very often that you see goat meat on a taco truck in Texas.

But you can't say that taco-truck food is entirely Americanized, either. Maria Rojas's tripe and sweet-breads tacos are exactly the kind of food that newly arrived immigrants will go out of their way for. These are the kind of tacos that might impress Mario Batali and Anthony Bourdain, who are big into offal dishes.

Since few of my dining companions like sweet-breads and tripe, I took my friend Bernard Brunon, an artist from France, to Taqueria Tacambaro. He was utterly amazed. And then he started taking other Frenchmen and visitors from France to eat tripe tacos there. Now photos of Taqueria Tacambaro are turning up in French art publications. I predict this taco trailer will someday be listed in French travel guides.

THE JARRO TACO TRAILER ON GESSner has become legendary among taco-truck owners. This is the most successful taco truck in the city. It does so much business that its owner, Guillermo "Memo" Piñedo, has opened a freestanding restaurant, called Jarro Café, right beside it.

There are guys who eat lunch at the trailer during the week, and then bring their families for a sit-down meal in the restaurant on the weekend. Jarro also serves tacos al pastor, made with marinated pork and the Yucatecan specialty, *cochinita pibíl*, which is marinated pork cooked in banana leaves. While you can get tacos al pastor at almost any taco truck in the city, the *bistec* (steak) tacos and the cochinita pibíl are unique. And so are the unusual salsas.

"There weren't any taco trucks around here when we started," said Memo when I ran into him at the trailer. "Now there are taco trucks all up and down Gessner." They are trying to duplicate Jarro's success. "But they don't get it. It's the quality of the food, not the location, that made this taco trailer successful," he said.

I sat down with Guillermo Piñedo and his wife for an interview. The couple once ran a three-location chain of Jarro Café restaurants in Mexico. The original location was in Mexico City, the other two were in the beach resort communities of Ixtapa and Cancún. The devaluation of

the peso in the Carlos Salinas era crippled their finances. Then Memo Piñedo was kidnapped.

"That was when we decided to get out," Señora Piñedo remembered.

The original idea was to come to Houston and open a restaurant. But the Piñedos didn't know much about the city, and that made it difficult to pick a location. The real estate negotiations, financing, and permit processes were also daunting. A friend of theirs who worked as a chef at a Houston restaurant suggested they consider a taco truck instead.

At first they dismissed the idea. They had never seen a taco truck in Mexico, so it was hard to imagine. But their friend drove them around to see a few in Houston and they began to realize the brilliance of the concept. If your location isn't working out, you move somewhere else, observed Memo.

The Piñedos invested $25,000 in a trailer and another $5,000 for everything else they needed. Their $30,000 investment was a tiny fraction of what it would cost to start a restaurant. And they had no loan payments to make. They paid several hundred dollars a month to rent a location in front of a liquor store on Gessner, but they had few other expenses.

Business was slow at first. "Memo only sold three kinds of tacos," said Señora Piñedo. "Steak, cochinita pibíl, and al pastor."

The *bistec* sold at most Houston Mexican restaurants is tough as shoe leather and riddled with gristle, so nobody was interested in a steak taco from a taco truck. And few of the laborers and immigrants who make up the majority of taco-truck customers had ever heard of the slow-cooked Mayan pork dish called cochinita pibíl.

"I ended up giving a lot of tacos away for free," Memo recalled.

And there were the weird salsas. Taco trucks, like taquerias, usually offer red and green sauce. Heat levels vary, but you seldom taste anything as hot as Jarro's orange chile de árbol or bright green serrano salsa in Houston. His friends pleaded with him to offer conventional fajita tacos and regular salsas, Memo recalled.

"Owners of other taco trucks asked me why I was paying two dollars a pound for sirloin when you could get fajita beef for a dollar a pound. I said,

OLD-FASHIONED TACO trucks inspired a new wave of cutting-edge street food from mobile kitchens such as Torchy's Tacos in Austin

'America has the best beef in the world, why not put it on a taco?' They thought I was crazy. But I wasn't going to sell what every other taco truck was selling," said Memo. "I was going to sell the kind of food we had at our restaurants in Mexico. I was going to do it my way."

Within three months, word of mouth about the sirloin tacos and the super-hot salsas had spread and the Jarro taco trailer on Gessner was swamped with customers. "I had to hire four workers to keep up with the orders," Memo said. Jarro taco-trailer workers all wear uniforms, and the trucks are sparkling clean and painted in striking black with very professional graphics.

Behind the Jarro Café, there are two brand-new taco trailers that Memo has recently ordered. He

5 GREAT TACO TRUCKS IN PORTLAND, OREGON

In 2007, the late great *Gourmet* magazine hired me to write a story about taco trucks across the country. I had already eaten at lots of taco trucks in the Southwest, but the story gave me a chance to sample food from taco trucks in Portland, Seattle, New York, and New Orleans.

I was shocked to discover how good the taco-truck food was in Portland, Oregon. Thanks to the artisan food movement, Portland liberalized health department regulations to allow certification of home kitchens. The same laws that made it possible for artisan bakers, chocolate makers, and canners to sell homemade wares at farmer's markets also made it possible for Portland taco trucks to sell Grandma's soup and pot roast.

Here are five of my favorite Portland taco trucks.

TACOS Y TORTAS MORELIA
FOSTER AND SE 52ND AVENUE
Don't miss Morelia's pambazo sandwich. The roll is dipped in dark dried chile sauce, then toasted on the griddle and stuffed with shredded homemade beef pot roast, cheese, potatoes, carrots, onions, lettuce, tomato, and sour cream. It's a whole pot roast dinner on a slippery chile-coated roll.

EL BRASERO
SE 12TH AVENUE AND HAWTHORNE BOULEVARD
On the El Brasero trailer, there is a sign that reads

MEXICO CITY–STYLE barbacoa at a trailer in Portland

RICA BARBACOA ESTILO D.F. That means Mexico City–style braised lamb shoulder cooked until it falls apart. It's served on corn tortillas and topped with chopped onion, cilantro, a squeeze of lime juice, and homemade green salsa. A Styrofoam cup of hot consommé comes on the side. Dip your taco in the hot spicy lamb broth and eat it while it is hot and drippy.

LINDO MICHOACAN
33RD AVENUE AND SE DIVISION STREET
The lusciously gelatinous braised beef cheek at the Lindo Michoacan truck at 33rd and Division tasted just like the Tex-Mex barbacoa we eat back home. I took my photo of the tacos at the communal picnic table nearby. This is the most popular taco truck in Portland and the most egalitarian. I watched a woman in a green designer coat and matching handbag get in line behind some Spanish-speaking guys in work boots, gimme caps, and sweatshirts to order lunch. I am sure the fresh handmade tortillas are part of the draw at Lindo Michoacan, but the fact that the truck is parked in a hip residential neighborhood close to downtown doesn't hurt, either.

LA CATRINA (TORTAS GIGANTES)
9694 SE 82ND AVENUE (NEAR OTTY) (BOB'S AUTO & GAS)
The ten-dollar *torta cubana* is a Mexican-style Cuban sandwich. It is only by virtue of the adhesive properties of melted American cheese that the layers of ham, steak Milanese, head cheese, scrambled eggs, a hot dog split into lengthwise quarters, tomato, avocado, pickles, jalapeños, and onions all stick together on the toasted bolillo. The sandwich is majestic.

MEXICO LINDO
ALOHA SHOPPING CENTER
18565 SW TUALATIN VALLEY HIGHWAY, ALOHA, OREGON
Try a foot-long flat taco called a *huarache* (it means "sandal" in Spanish) at the Mexico Lindo truck in the parking lot of the Aloha Shopping Center. You can barely see the refried beans and grilled meats on top of the freshly made masa (corn dough) for all the lettuce, tomato, radishes, white cheese, and sour cream on top.

intends to expand his brand with franchisees. Why franchise taco trailers instead of restaurants? "Because the trailers are cheaper, easier to run, and more profitable," Memo said.

"It's crazy to have a taco trailer out front in the parking lot competing with your restaurant, huh?" Memo said with a laugh. But there's no way he would close it. The trailer makes as much money as the restaurant.

Why don't the taco-trailer customers come inside?

"There are lots of reasons," Memo explained. Some loyal outdoor customers are laborers who don't have time to change clothes and clean up. It's also faster outside, and it's twenty-five-cents-a-taco cheaper.

"It's my drive-through window," he joked.

PINK'S HOT Dogs in Los Angeles started out as a pushcart in 1939

THE SUPER TACOS TRUCK AT NINETY-sixth and Broadway on the island of Manhattan has been in the same spot for almost twenty years. "It used to be an older truck, and it used to be only tacos," a customer who was waiting in line told me. He had been eating here for twelve years. I ordered the dinner special, which was chicken in mole sauce, six tacos with various meats, and two sopes.

Then I hailed a cab and climbed into the back seat with my large white sack. I had told Jane Daniels Lear, then my editor at *Gourmet,* that to wrap up my taco-truck article, I would pick up dinner at a Manhattan taco truck for her and her husband. As I headed across town to her fashionable East Side apartment, I began to question my sanity. I had never eaten anything from the Super Tacos truck before. What if the food wasn't any good? What if I poisoned her?

For a long time, Super Tacos was the only taco truck on the entire island of Manhattan. In 2006, another one, called Taco Express, moved to 145th Street in Harlem. But it was a third truck, called El Ídolo, from Corona, Queens, that got all the attention. It started swooping into Manhattan late at night and parking on Eighth Avenue and Fourteenth Street in the trendy Meatpacking District when the bars were closing. Hip young New Yorkers got a taste, and suddenly taco trucks were the buzz. Now they are all over New York.

"Taco trucks are adored because they are totally unpretentious," Manhattan Mexican chef Aaron Sanchez told me. "You eat with your hands." Sanchez, who authored *La Comida del Barrio,* used to frequent the taco trucks in his hometown of El Paso. In New York, he likes a trailer called Taco Guicho at Roosevelt Avenue and Eighty-fourth Street in Queens for the sopes.

When I got to my editor's place, I unloaded the sack and arranged the goodies on wooden cutting boards so we could split them at the table. There was so much ohhing and ahhing that I figured I was pretty much off the hook.

Taco trucks are popping up all over, and their impact should not be underestimated. At first glance, the taco truck seems like a fusion of modern American automotive culture and inexpensive Mexican street food. But in fact, the taco truck is a Trojan horse.

What they are sneaking in is the invasive culture of *antojitos,* those inexpensive, satisfying corn-based snacks topped with grilled meats and chile sauces. Once you start eating this stuff, you're hooked.

Taquero-Style Tacos

VARIATION

GRIDDLE-ROASTED CHILE PEPPERS, TOMATOES, AND ONION SLICES

A good taquero doesn't waste grill space. When you are going to grill some meat or fish outside on the grill, bring along some whole, fresh jalapeños or serranos, tomatoes, and onion slices and roast them on the grill in a frying pan placed on the grill while the rest of the food is cooking.

YOU CAN USE ANY RECIPE FOR MEAT, SEAFOOD, OR GRILLED vegetables in this book as a taco filling. Freshly made tortillas are the ultimate taco wrappers, but taco truck–style tacos are usually made by wrapping one or two commercial tortillas around the filling.

Vegetable oil
Corn tortillas

Flour tortillas can be heated dry, corn tortillas need a little oil and steam to soften and make them pliable. Two thin commercial corn tortillas are often stuck together for each taco. The skillful taquero will lay the corn tortillas on the griddle on or near the meat or fish in order to catch some of the oil and juices, using these to soften the tortilla and add to the flavor. Finish the heating by flipping the lightly oiled corn tortillas on the hot griddle a few times to crisp them up.

Grilled onions are frequently mixed in with the grilled meat. The standard garnish is Onion and Cilantro (page 169). Chopped radishes, chopped tomato, and shredded lettuce are also common.

Griddle-roasted chile peppers are often offered on the side.

Filet Mignon Tacos

MAKES 8 TACOS

THIS RECIPE WAS INSPIRED BY MEMO'S SHAVED STEAK TACOS at his Jarro taco trailer. Memo shaves his sirloin on a meat slicer, but here's another way to get thin steak slices. Those inexpensive little bacon-wrapped filet mignons that come in individual plastic packages are perfect for this.

Two 6-ounce filet mignons
¼ cup freshly squeezed lemon juice
¼ cup olive oil
4 cloves garlic, minced
2 tablespoons New Mexican chile powder or other pure chile powder
Sea salt to taste

FOR SERVING
1 cup All-American Guacamole (page 197)
8 tortillas (see Taquero-Style Tacos, page 164)
4 tomato slices
½ cup crumbled Mexican white cheese
8 black olives, sliced
4 sprigs fresh cilantro
Bottled hot sauces

Slice the filets in half to form 4 round medallions. Slice in half again to form 8 circles of beef. On a flat work surface, cover each with cellophane or wax paper and pound with the flat side of a meat cleaver to form a thin round about a ¼ inch thick and 3 inches across. Don't overdo it; you don't want the meat to fall apart. Combine the lemon juice, olive oil, garlic, and chile powder in a bowl large enough to accommodate the meat and mix well. Place the meat in the bowl and cover with the marinade, turning well to coat. Place in the refrigerator for 30 minutes or so.

Prepare the grill. Grill the beef over a hot fire until done to taste; this will only take a minute or two for medium-rare. Slice each beef medallion into thin strips and salt to taste. Spread ⅛ cup guacamole evenly on each tortilla. Top with a tomato slice and beef strips and sprinkle crumbled cheese over the meat. Garnish with olives and cilantro. Serve immediately with a selection of bottled hot sauces.

HOUSTON'S
TOP 5 TACO TRUCKS

#1 JARRO CAFÉ
IN FRONT OF JARRO CAFÉ
1521 GESSNER DRIVE

What to get: Don't miss the steak (bistec) taco made with thin-sliced Angus sirloin. Also recommended: the Campechana (beef and chorizo), cochinita pibíl (slow-cooked pork), and beef-and-mushroom tacos. Flour tortillas are available for a little extra. Don't miss the salsa bar. The dark-green jalapeño-and-cilantro salsa may be the mildest; the dried chile salsa is complex and picante. Only the most dedicated chile-heads should attempt to ingest the incendiary orange chile de árbol sauce and the rip-your-lips-off neon green serrano slurry. The food is a little cheaper and a little faster at the taco trailer, but they have the same tacos inside the air-conditioned restaurant, where you also get chips, ice water, knives and forks, and an expanded menu.

#2 TAQUERIA TACAMBARO
2520 AIRLINE DRIVE (BEHIND CANINO'S)

What to get: Tacos de mollejas and tripitas (sweetbreads and tripe) are amazing. If you don't like offal, try the spicy pork al pastor, crisped up in a frying pan and served with raw onion and cilantro, and the awesome gordita, made with a thick masa cake split in half, then stuffed with homemade refried beans and Mexican cheese. Don't miss the roasted jalapeños. Mexican nationals come from miles around to eat Maria Rojas's home-style Michoacán cooking.

#3 EL ULTIMO
7403 LONG POINT ROAD
(SOUTHWEST CORNER OF LONG POINT ROAD AND ANTOINE DRIVE)

Look for a shiny new taco truck parked in front of a car wash. The sanitary standards are exceptional. Both the man and woman behind the counter were wearing hair nets. What to get: The breakfast tacos are a dollar apiece, and they're huge. They come with your choice of scrambled eggs with bacon, ham, potatoes, nopalitos, *machacado* (shredded beef), chorizo, or roasted peppers on a corn or flour tortilla. The flour tortillas are handmade, and the chorizo is truly exceptional. The thick green salsa is pretty hot and the red is a little tamer. There's no coffee, but there are fresh-fruit aguas frescas available. Don't be suprised if the truck isn't there; it goes to the commissary for cleaning and restocking frequently.

#4 EL NORTEÑO
LONG POINT ROAD AND GESSNER DRIVE

This is a "chain" with a couple of blue school buses and at least one blue trailer. They change locations often, but they can usually be found around the corner of Gessner and Long Point. At this writing, there is a blue bus on Gessner north of Long Point and a blue "El Norteño" truck out in front of the shopping center at 9893 Long Point. What to get: Pollo asado estilo Monterrey is their specialty—six dollars for half a chicken, ten dollars for a whole one. Both come with tortillas, a roasted onion, chiles, and condiments. The chicken is good, but *costillas al carbón*—a whole slab of grilled spare ribs with onions, chiles, and condiments for fifteen dollars—are even better. A half slab, which goes for $7.50, is more than enough for two.

#5 TACOS TIERRA CALIENTE
1300 BLOCK OF MONTROSE BOULEVARD IN THE "WE FIX FLATS" PARKING LOT

Maria Samano and her flirtatious crew from the "hotlands" of Michoacán run this extremely popular taco trailer in the Montrose. What to get: barbacoa tacos with onions and cilantro. Ask Maria for the "salsita," and she'll hand you a squirt bottle full of her creamy green "hotlands hot sauce."

EL ULTIMO taco truck in Houston serves awesome breakfast tacos

Sweetbread Tacos

MAKES 8 TACOS

MARIA ROJAS AT THE TAQUERIA TACAMBARO TRUCK GAVE me her mollejas (sweetbreads) recipe. She said to boil the sweetbreads in salted water until slightly firm, break them apart, and grill them on a flat top with no oil or seasonings. You season the mollejas with salsa when you make the tacos, she told me.

After experimenting, I adapted the recipe to the Argentine grilling style. Mollejas are always among the first things you are served at a traditional South American asado. The chimichurri gives the sweetbreads more flavor.

1 to 1½ pounds beef mollejas (sweetbreads)
1 tablespoon salt
1 cup vinegar
Tex-Mex Chimichurri (page 93)
Six 6-inch wooden skewers, soaked in water for 15 minutes

FOR SERVING
8 tortillas (see Taquero-Style Tacos, page 164)
Onions and Cilantro (page 169)
Salsa of your choice

Soak the mollejas in cold water for 30 minutes. Drain the water. Slit the membrane in the center so the mollejas lie flat. Cover the mollejas in more cold water in a medium saucepan and add the salt and vinegar. Bring the water to a boil over high heat. Turn the heat down and simmer for 5 to 10 minutes, until the lobes are translucent but still soft.

Plunge the blanched sweetbreads into cold water. Cut off all excess membrane with a sharp knife. Break up the mollejas into 1- to 1½-inch pieces. Cut off as much membrane as you can easily remove. Place the pieces in a resealable plastic bag and add the Tex-Mex Chimichurri, turning to coat evenly. Marinate for an hour or more in the refrigerator.

Light the grill. Put the pieces of mollejas on soaked wooden skewers. Grill over medium-high heat, turning until nicely browned on all sides, about 4 minutes. Do not overcook.

To serve, chop the sweetbreads, removing any remaining membrane, and divide among the tortillas with a topping of Onions and Cilantro and the salsa of your choice.

Onions and Cilantro

MAKES ½ CUP

THIS IS THE TACO GARNISH SERVED AT NEARLY EVERY TACO truck and taqueria in Texas.

- ½ cup chopped onions
- 1 tablespoon minced fresh cilantro
- Juice of one lime

Combine ingredients in a bowl and mix well. Use immediately and make more as needed; the mixture doesn't stay fresh very long.

TACOS GABY'S, NEW ORLEANS

The Tacos Gaby's truck was parked on Hope Street, near the Lowe's building-supply store on the edge of the French Quarter. The taco truck's customers, most of them laborers on lunch break, sat in folding chairs or on the curb.

After Katrina, an army of Spanish-speaking immigrants arrived in New Orleans to rebuild the city, causing stand-up comic George Lopez to quip that FEMA stood for "find every Mexican available." The sudden arrival of a major Latin American population in New Orleans was a fast-motion version of the immigration pattern that's taken place in other cities and towns over the course of decades.

Wearing a baseball cap and eating a quesadilla al pastor on the curb by the Tacos Gaby's truck was chef John Currence from City Grocery in Oxford, Mississippi. Currence is a New Orleans native and he spent an enormous amount of time doing volunteer work in New Orleans after Katrina.

"For a good while after the hurricane, the taco trucks were the only places to eat," said Currence. "It's honest, handmade food, and it's a dollar twenty-five a taco." The grilled meats, hot-off-the-griddle tortillas, and fresh pico de gallo served at the taco trucks was a huge improvement over what used to pass for Mexican food in New Orleans.

I struck up a conversation with the twenty-two-year-old man who was running the taco truck. He told me he had traveled to New Orleans two months after Katrina hit. He had found plenty of construction work, but nothing to eat. So he had called his parents, who operated a taco truck in Houston, and told them to come to New Orleans. They brought the truck over and business was so good, the whole family decided to relocate. They have lived here ever since. They still take the truck back to Houston to buy groceries and Mexican sodas.

IN MEXICO City, *tacos al pastor* are made from pork that is cut from a revolving "trompo" of meat on a vertical roaster

Tacos al Pastor

MAKES 12 TACOS

CITY HEALTH DEPARTMENTS IN THE UNITED STATES HAVE outlawed tacos al pastor because the pork on the vertical roaster is uncooked. Here's a recipe that captures the same flavor.

¼ cup granulated garlic
1 tablespoon cider vinegar
1 teaspoon dried oregano
1 teaspoon powdered chile
1 teaspoon freshly ground black pepper
Pinch of ground cumin
Salt
2 cups freshly squeezed orange juice
1 tablespoon achiote paste (optional)
2 pounds boneless pork loin, thinly sliced
½ pineapple, peeled, cored, and cut into long, thick strips

FOR SERVING
12 tortillas (see Taquero-Style Tacos, page 164), warmed
Onions and Cilantro (page 169)
Picante Sauce (page 218)

In a medium bowl, combine the garlic, vinegar, oregano, chile powder, black pepper, cumin, salt to taste, orange juice, and achiote paste, if using. Add the pork slices and turn to coat both sides. Marinate for at least 1 hour.

Heat the grill. Place the meat over hot coals and cook, turning once and basting with any leftover marinade during cooking, until crisp. At the same time, grill the pineapple strips, turning as needed, until lightly browned.

To assemble, chop the grilled pork into ¼-inch pieces. Cut the pineapple into ½-inch pieces. Place the pork on the warmed tortillas and top with Onions and Cilantro and pineapple pieces. Serve the Picante Sauce on the side.

Tex-Mex Quesadillas

MAKES 4 QUESADILLAS

VARIATIONS

DELUXE QUESADILLAS

Put 1 cheese-topped tortilla on the bottom and one without cheese on the top and proceed as directed, omitting the foldover step. Cut the finished quesadilla into quarters with a sharp knife. Garnish with guacamole and cilantro.

GRILLED QUESADILLAS

You can also heat quesadillas on the grill grate, but be careful to make sure the cheese has melted and is holding the contents in place before you flip it over.

A QUESADILLA IS A GRILLED CHEESE SANDWICH MADE WITH tortillas. In Texas, quesadillas are made with flour tortillas. (In Mexico, corn tortillas are used.)

- 4 ounces grated jack cheese, mozzarella, or shredded Oaxacan string cheese
- 4 flour tortillas
- 4 teaspoons butter
- 4 ounces meat filling, hot (optional)

Divide the cheese evenly among the 4 flour tortillas. On a hot flat top or comal, melt the butter over medium heat. When the butter starts to bubble, add the cheese-topped tortillas. Toast for about 2 minutes, or until the cheese begins to melt. Divide the filling, if using, among the tortillas and fold them over so the filling is sandwiched in the hot cheese. Continue cooking until the tortilla gets brown and crisp. Serve the quesadillas piping hot.

Tortas

TORTAS ARE MADE ON *TELERA* BREAD, A SIX- TO EIGHT-INCH roll sold in Mexican bakeries. Be sure to buy your telera rolls the same day you plan to make the sandwiches or keep them in the freezer; they go stale very quickly. A sandwich made on a whole telera roll is usually sold as a gigante or giant-size sandwich. Half a telera roll makes a regular-size sandwich. If you can't find telera bread, you can substitute torpedo rolls or kaiser rolls.

Chicken, steak, and roast pork are all common fillings; so are hot dogs cut lengthwise into thin slices and grilled. A fried egg is a favorite addition. Be creative. You can use any meat or combination of meats for the sandwich filling; just slice the meat into easy-to-eat slivers or thin pieces.

> 2 large telera rolls (or substitute torpedo rolls)
> 4 slices muenster or provolone cheese
> ½ cup Refried Beans (page 204)

> **FILLINGS OF YOUR CHOICE**
> 4 well-done fried eggs (optional)
> 4 thin tomato slices
> 4 thin onion slices
> ¼ cup mayonnaise (in a squeeze bottle if possible)
> Pickled Jalapeño slices (page 227), optional
> 1 large avocado, thinly sliced

Prepare the grill. Separate the rolls and toast them on the grill, cut side down, while the meat is cooking (or reheating). Turn the telera bread over crust side down and place two cheese slices on each top bun. Close the lid of the grill and allow the cheese to melt. Spread ¼ cup Refried Beans on each toasted bottom bun and top with fillings. Add two fried eggs side by side, if desired. Put a couple tomato slices and two onion slices over the fillings and squiggle or dot with mayo. Add a couple slices of jalapeño if desired. Divide the avocado slices among the toasted top buns and push them into the cheese. Clamp the top buns onto the bottoms and compress lightly so the sandwiches hold together. Slice in half and serve hot.

THE SANDWICH maker at this Matamoros *torta* shop cuts the *tortas* in half with an electric knife on the flat top

Norteño Pollo Asado

SERVES 2 TO 4

NORTEÑO POLLO ASADO, THE STYLE OF MESQUITE-GRILLED chicken popular in Monterrey and the north of Mexico, is one of the most common taco-truck offerings in Texas—only the taco trucks are usually school buses fitted with mesquite grills. Mesquite wood or mesquite charcoal is a must for this recipe.

8 cups hot water
½ cup sea salt
3 tablespoons Tabasco or other hot sauce (or more to taste)
1 tablespoon freshly ground black pepper
1 tablespoon poultry seasoning
1 can beer
1 whole fryer chicken, 3 to 4 pounds
Oil, for frying
¼ cup Red Rub (page 24)
3 cups Italian dressing such as Wishbone

In a large bowl or crock that will fit in your refrigerator, stir the water, salt, hot sauce, pepper, and poultry seasoning together, making sure the salt is dissolved. Add the beer. Cool the mixture down in the refrigerator.

Remove the giblets and with a sharp knife or poultry shears, cut the chicken along the backbone and flatten it open to butterfly it. Rinse the insides. Submerge the chicken in the brine, placing a weight on top of it to keep it submerged. Keep it in the refrigerator for 24 hours to cure. To check the spice and salt level, heat a little oil in a frying pan, cut off a piece of chicken, and cook it on both sides.

Light a grill using mesquite charcoal or mesquite wood burned down to coals. Remove the chicken from the brine; pat dry. When the chicken is dry, rub it with Red Rub. Spread the butterflied chicken on the grill, bone side down, and cook covered with indirect heat for 3 hours, mopping with Italian dressing every 30 minutes.

Cook to an internal temperature of 165°F. Serve with tortillas and with condiments of your choice.

Tangerine Chicken

SERVES 2 TO 4

MARINATING CHICKEN IN MEXICAN SODA SWEETENED WITH cane sugar is a popular technique at Latino food stands that serve roasted chicken. To avoid messing up the refrigerator, I use two half-gallon plastic drink pitchers; each holds half a chicken and half the marinade.

1.5 liters Jarritos Mandarin soda (1 large bottle)
4 cloves garlic
½ cup sea salt
4 bay leaves
2 serrano chiles, cut in half lengthwise
10 peppercorns
2 half chickens, 1 chicken cut in 8 pieces, or 4 leg quarters
¼ cup Red Rub (page 24)

VARIATION

For tamarind chicken, use Jarritos Tamarind soda, or use any other cane-sugar-sweetened soda that sounds like it would be a complement to roasted chicken.

Combine all ingredients except the chicken and the rub in a large nonreactive container (or two half-gallon plastic drink pitchers with tight lids). Add the chicken pieces, cover, and marinate in the refrigerator for 48 to 72 hours. Test the flavor and salt level by cutting off a small piece and cooking it. If the chicken has reached the desired salt level, but you aren't ready to cook it yet, just pour off the marinade.

Prepare the grill. Season the chicken with the Red Rub and sear on the hottest part of the grill skin side down until well browned. Move the chicken to medium heat and cook, turning often, until the juices run clear when the thigh is punctured, 45 minutes to an hour for half chickens or 20 to 30 minutes for pieces.

TACOS EL ASADERO, SEATTLE

It was a blustery day in Seattle when I climbed aboard the big white school bus called Tacos El Asadero on Rainier Avenue South. There I found people seated on round stools at stainless-steel counters that ran along both sides of the front half of the bus. The kitchen and the cashier's stand were in the back.

Taco trucks change their shapes and sizes to suit their locales. In Texas, where pick-up trucks are common, the taco trailer is becoming increasingly popular. In New York, where parking is a nightmare, the taco pushcart has emerged. And in rainy Se-

attle, taco lovers sit inside a "taco bus" to stay out of the rain.

I called chef Jesse Thomas of the Crow Restaurant and Bar when I got to town and asked him about Seattle taco trucks. The taco trucks started arriving in Seattle about six years ago, Thomas told me. And Seattle chefs were among the first to embrace them. "You line up with the workmen to eat. And that's a beautiful thing," he said. "One of my favorite things to do on my day off is go sit in the [El Asadero] taco bus."

THE HAMBURGER patties at Hamburguesas Del Rio in Monterrey are seasoned with garlic salt and Worcestershire sauce and mixed with bread crumbs and eggs

Hamburguesas

TO UNDERSTAND EXACTLY WHAT the term *hamburguesa estilo Monterrey* meant, I visited the Hamburguesas Del Rio location at Avenida Constitución 1121 Pte. Centro in Monterrey. From the Monterrey-style burgers I'd had in Houston, I assumed that the term described a specific set of garnishes, namely a white-bread bun topped with shredded lettuce, chopped onion, sliced tomato, then a hamburger patty, a slice of ham, and sliced avocado.

But I was wrong. A couple of bites revealed that there was something altogether different about the hamburger patty itself. So I asked the *hamburguesero* what went into the meat mix. *Migas* (bread crumbs), *huevos* (eggs), and garlic salt were among the ingredients he named. I have since found recipes online that include those items as well as salsa inglés (Worcestershire), soy sauce, and other seasonings.

When you order a hamburguesa from a taco truck or taqueria in Houston, you usually get an Americanized version of the hamburguesa estilo Monterrey: regular all-beef hamburger patties dressed with slices of ham and avocados in addition to the usual lettuce, tomato, and mayonnaise. It's an excellent adaptation.

You find lots of other Latino burger variations in Texas, too, including the green chile cheese-burger of El Paso, the bean burger of San Antonio, and Mexico City's *hamburguesa estilo D.F.,* which comes with ham and a pineapple slice on top of the burger patty. The *hamburguesa torta,* or "tortaburger" that's served on taco trucks and at taquerias often comes on fresh-baked telera bread (see recipe on page 183).

Unfortunately, most Latino burgers come with thin, flavorless, previously frozen burger patties cooked well done. That's a problem that's easy to fix when you make them in your backyard. Put one of your own big fat homemade burger patties in these recipes and you'll have a helluva Tex-Mex burger in your hands.

Homemade Ground Meats While it sounds like a big project, the truth is making your own ground meat is pretty simple—if you have a meat grinder. You can grind venison, wild boar, duck, or other game and use it in all kinds of recipes without paying a lot of money to a wild game processor, too.

When grinding your own beef, look for chuck, round, brisket, or sirloin that's on the fatty side. If you make the Tex-Mex Churrrasco on page 92 you will find yourself with around three pounds of fatty tenderloin trimmings that are perfect for this purpose. Likewise you will get a lot of trimmings if you cut your own rib-eye steaks.

But if you are using chuck or round, odds are you won't be close to a 70:30 meat to fat ratio. Which is why you will probably want to supplement the fat content of your ground meat. There are lots of ways to do this: you can add beef fat, salt pork, or any variety of fat you can find. But my favorite method was devised by the late great Tookie's, a hamburger joint in Seabrook, Texas, that was closed by Hurricane Ike in 2008.

Tookie's "Squealer" was a burger with bacon ground up with the beef. It's easy enough to throw a few slices of bacon in the grinder if you are grinding up your own hamburger meat anyway. And you'll love the flavor.

SOMETIMES TACO truck *hamburguesas* come on hamburger buns, and sometimes they come *torta*-style on *telera* bread

Tookie's Ground Beef

MAKES AROUND 2 POUNDS

2 pounds chuck, round, or sirloin
6 ounces bacon

VARIATIONS
TWO-MEAT BLEND
Use 1 pound beef and 1 pound venison, lamb, or goat meat along with the bacon.

Remove ligament, silver skin, or any other tough pieces and discard. Cut the meat into strips. Run the beef strips and bacon through a meat grinder. Combine well with your hands to spread the bacon fat evenly through the beef. Use immediately, keep tightly wrapped in the refrigerator for a few days, or freeze.

HAMBURGER HELP

Grocery stores label ground beef with a ratio of meat to fat. "80-20" means 80 percent meat, 20 percent fat. You need fat to keep your burger juicy. The idea that lean meat is somehow superior has really messed up the hamburgers in this country. It's not unusual to see "90-10" ground sirloin or even "93-7" in the grocery store. With so little fat, this kind of meat dries out quickly on the grill—especially if you take the USDA's advice and cook your burgers to 160°F.

Old-time butchers used to recommend a 70:30 ratio for a really juicy burger, and chefs in fine-dining restaurants are reviving this practice. Chef Bryan Caswell in Houston told me he started making the tiny hamburgers called sliders as bar snacks to use up his fatty rib-eye steak trimmings. The sliders became so popular Caswell now has two slider restaurants called Little Bigs in addition to Reef, his award-winning Houston fine-dining restaurant.

If you like your burgers rare, Caswell recommends that you grind your own burger meat (see Homemade Ground Meats, page 179). Top chefs who love burgers also recommend that you hand-pack well-seasoned, fatty burger meat at the last minute. Flip it as seldom as possible. And most importantly, resist the temptation to push down on top of the burger patty with a spatula, because doing so will force all the juices out.

Trevino's Chile-Cheese Stuffed Burgers

MAKES SIX ½-POUND BURGERS OR EIGHT ⅓-POUND BURGERS

JAMES BEARD HATED REGULAR CHEESEBURGERS. IN *AMERI-can Cookery,* he offered his own recipe with one cup of cheddar, gruyère, or blue cheese mixed with two pounds of ground meat along with Worcestershire, Tabasco, minced garlic, and salt. The result was far superior to a conventional cheeseburger, in Beard's view. That's the way Jacob Trevino and lots of other Texas tailgaters are doing it these days, too.

1 cup shredded jack cheese, divided
1 teaspoon minced green chile, or fresh or Pickled Jalapeños (page 227)
3 pounds ground beef
1 envelope Lipton onion soup mix
2.25-ounce can chopped black olives
1 tablespoon Worcestershire sauce
1 egg, lightly beaten
¼ cup grated parmesan cheese

Divide the jack cheese in half. Mix ½ cup with the minced chiles and set aside for the stuffing.

In a large mixing bowl, combine the ground beef with the remaining ingredients and the other half of the shredded cheese. Divide the meat into balls. (Six balls will weigh just over ½ pound each; eight balls will come out to around ⅓ pound each.) With your thumb, create a pocket in the center of each ball. Force ⅛ cup of the chile-cheese mixture into the pocket. Now seal the burger meat around the stuffing and flatten the ball into a patty.

Prepare the grill. Cook the burgers to the desired level of doneness, flipping as seldom as possible to keep the cheese from escaping through a crack in the patty. Serve the patties on toasted hamburger buns or telera bread with your favorite condiments.

Tex-Mex Burger Patties

MAKES FOUR ½-POUND OR SIX ⅓-POUND PATTIES

VARIATION

TEX-MEX CHEESEBURGER PATTIES

Add ½ cup grated jack, cheddar, or other cheese and proceed as directed.

START WITH GROUND CHUCK OR GROUND ROUND WITH A HIGH fat content—at least 20 percent fat to 80 percent meat (see box on page 180). Pack the burgers by hand and don't compress them too much or try too hard to make them perfectly round. A patty with a few uneven edges produces a burger with an interesting texture.

> 2 pounds ground beef
> 1 tablespoon Tex-Mex Grill Blend (page 21)
> 1 tablespoon minced garlic
> 1 tablespoon minced serrano chile
> 1 teaspoon Worcestershire sauce

Combine all of the ingredients and mix well. Form into patties. If you plan on freezing some, separate the patties with wax paper so you can remove as many as you need.

TO MAKE a stuffed cheeseburger, make a pocket in the patty and put some extra cheese or other stuffings in the middle, then seal it back up

Tortaburgers

MAKES 4 SINGLE-PORTION BURGER TORTAS OR 2 GIGANTE BURGER TORTAS

TELERA BREAD IS THE LARGE FLAT ROLL SOLD IN MEXICAN bakeries that's used to make the sandwiches called tortas. Telera bread makes an exceptional hamburger roll. Be sure to buy your telera the same day you plan to make the burgers or keep it in the freezer; it goes stale very quickly.

Getting your hamburger patty to fit the oversize telera bread roll is the big challenge of making tortaburgers. Most torta shops flatten the ground meat very thin to cover the whole roll. I've given up on this approach for several reasons. First, it's difficult to cook a large, thin patty without breaking it. And it seems no matter how big I make my raw hamburger patty it shrinks on the grill to half the size of the roll. Most importantly, I don't like thin hamburger patties.

I think the best idea is to put two regular burger patties on each roll. Sandwich shops like Torta El Angel in Houston offer your choice of regular or gigante. At my house, we call the half telera bun with one burger patty on it a "regular" tortaburger and the whole telera bread with double burger patties a "gigante."

    2 large telera bread rolls
    4 slices Swiss or provolone cheese
    4 Tex-Mex Burger Patties, size of your choice (page 182)
    ½ cup Refried Beans (page 204)
    4 well-done fried eggs (optional)
    4 thin tomato slices
    4 thin onion slices
    ½ cup mayonnaise (in a squeeze bottle if possible)
    Pickled jalapeño slices (see page 227)
    1 large avocado, thinly sliced

Prepare the grill. Separate the rolls and toast them cut side down on the grill while the burgers are cooking. Turn the rolls over crust side down and place two cheese slices on each top bun. Close the lid of grill and allow the cheese to melt. Cook the burger patties to your preferred degree of doneness. Spread Refried Beans on each toasted bottom bun and top with two cooked burger patties side by side. Center the fried eggs on the burger patties, if using. Put a tomato slice and an onion slice on each patty and squiggle or dot with mayo. Add a couple slices of jalapeño. Divide the avocado slices among the toasted top buns and push them into the cheese. Clamp the top bun onto the bottom and compress lightly so the sandwich holds together. Slice in between the burger patties.

THIS TINY storefront on the side of a busy Monterrey street offered fresh eggs, hot dogs, hamburgers, tostadas, and Pepsi

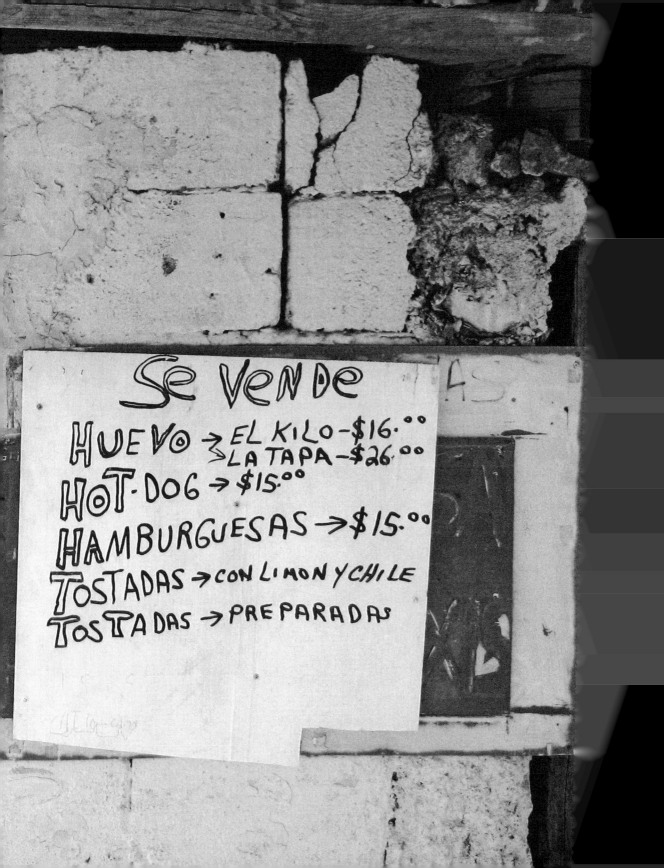

Hamburguesa Estilo Monterrey

Makes 4

THIS IS THE CLASSIC NORTHERN MEXICAN–STYLE HAMBURGER, minus the bread crumbs and fillers.

4 Tex-Mex Burger Patties, size of your choice (page 182)
4 hamburger buns
2 tablespoons butter
½ cup mayonnaise
1 cup shredded lettuce
½ cup finely chopped onion
4 large tomato slices
4 thin slices ham
1 large avocado, thinly sliced
Pickled jalapeño slices (see page 227), optional

Prepare the grill. Cook the burger patties to your preferred degree of doneness. Separate the buns, butter them lightly, and toast them on the grill while the burgers are cooking. Spread mayo on each toasted bottom bun and top with lettuce, onion, and tomato. Place one cooked burger on top of the vegetables on each bottom bun. Top the burger with the ham. Divide the avocado slices among the four toasted top buns and spread until the avocado adheres. Put the jalapeño slices on top of the ham if you're adding them, and then clamp the top bun onto the burger and compress lightly so the sandwich holds together.

San Antonio Bean Burgers

MAKES 4

YOU CAN USE EITHER HALF-POUND OR THIRD-POUND BURGER patties for these. For half-pound burgers, you need large buns. Don't skip the corn chips; they are the key to the bean burger's texture. I like jalapeño slices on top, but some folks prefer salsa.

    4 Tex-Mex Burger Patties, size of your choice (page 182)
    4 hamburger buns
    1 cup warm Refried Beans (page 204)
    Medium-size bag of corn chips (such as Fritos)
    Pickled jalapeño slices (see page 227) or salsa of your choice
    1 cup Chile con Queso (page 198) or Cheez Whiz
    ¼ onion, minced

Prepare the grill. Cook the burger patties to your preferred degree of doneness. Separate the buns and toast them on the grill while the burgers are cooking. Spread warm beans on the bottom bun and shove a handful of corn chips into the beans so they stick. Put the burger patty on top. Add slices of jalapeño or a spoonful of salsa, if desired. Spread the top bun generously with Chile con Queso or Cheez Whiz, sprinkle with the minced onion, and quickly place on top of the burger. Compress lightly so that the burger holds together. Serve immediately.

BEAN BURGERS

The most unique Tex-Mex burger is the San Antonio bean burger. In his book *Hamburgers and Fries*, John T. Edge devotes an entire chapter to the San Antonio invention. The bean burger and its Tex-Mex embellishments "define the burger as Texan, while paying homage to the Mexican roots of the state's people," Edge wrote. He goes on to compare the bean burger's sense of place with that of Washington State's cedar-planked salmon.

Tex-Mex bean burgers should not be confused with California's vegetarian bean burgers, in which beans are a replacement for the meat. The San Antonio bean burger is a regular hamburger patty with refried beans studded with Fritos corn chips. The original, which was invented at Sill's Snack Shack

in 1953, was then topped with Cheez Whiz and raw onions. There are many variations.

The Fritos sound like a terrible idea, but they make the bean burger sing. The soft beans and crunchy corn chips add a new level of textural interest to the hamburger. And Fritos were invented in San Antonio, after all. There are a lot of ways to go with the cheese. Most hamburger joints that make bean burgers use American or cheddar these days.

At Mama's Café in San Antonio, the beans and Fritos are on the bottom bun, then comes a thick slice of purple onion. Next comes a quarter-pound burger patty topped with a standard square of American cheese. Guacamole and salsa are served in plastic cups on the side so you can add them or not as you prefer.

Sonoran Hot Dogs

MAKES 4

AT MONTERREY-STYLE MEXICAN RESTAURANTS THESE ARE made with fat red hot dogs and are called *salchichas rojos*. In Tuscon, they are called Sonoran hot dogs. Tuscon hot dog vendors keep their mayo in squeeze bottles so they can apply it in decorative squiggles. There are all sorts of variations, but the bacon-wrapped wiener is essential. Look for a small size *bolillo* or torpedo roll to keep the bread-to-meat ratio in line. If refried beans, avocado, cheese, salsa, onions, and mayo seems like a lot of stuff to put on a hot dog, consider the Brazilian hot dog, which adds peas, corn, carrots, and crunchy potato sticks, too.

    4 teaspoons mayonnaise
    1 teaspoon Tabasco or other hot sauce
    Juice of 1 lemon
    4 all-beef wieners (fat ones work better than long ones)
    4 slices extra-thin bacon
    4 torpedo rolls or bolillos
    4 tablespoons warm Refried Beans (page 204)
    8 tablespoons chopped avocado (or guacamole) (see page 197)
    4 heaping tablespoons grated jack or cheddar cheese or
        substitute Chile con Queso (page 198)
    4 tablespoons chopped onion
    4 tablespoons chopped tomato
    4 tablespoons Salsa Verde (page 219)

Mix the mayo, Tabasco, and lemon juice and use a funnel to put the mayo blend in a squeeze bottle. Wrap the wieners with the bacon slices so the sausage is completely covered. Cook the wieners on a comal or flat top, rolling them over until the bacon is crunchy on all sides, about 7 minutes. Cut a pocket into the buns to form a "boat" and toast them on the grill. When the wieners are cooked, divide the beans and avocado among the four rolls, spooning them inside the pocket and spreading on either side. Spread the cheese down the middle. Using tongs, put one piping-hot bacon-wrapped wiener into the pocket of each roll. Top each wiener with onions and tomatoes. Spread the Salsa Verde across the top. Apply the mayo blend in squiggles across the top of the hot dog.

THE SONORAN hot dog
at James Coney Island
in Houston starts with
a frankfurter wrapped
in bacon

LYNDON JOHNSON
celebrating the opening
of the Cordova Bridge,
connecting El Paso and
Juárez, 1959

CHAPTER 9

BICULTURAL BEANS AND BORDER SIDES

FROM A DISTANCE, THE BORDER WHERE TEXAS ENDS and Mexico begins seems distinct. When you get there, it all becomes fuzzy. Every morning hordes of American retirees cross the bridges from Texas into Mexico to buy cheap prescriptions in Mexican drug stores. And in the other direction, waves of Mexicans enter the United States, to convert their pesos into dollars and deposit them in American banks as a hedge against devaluation of the peso. International trade has made the Lower Rio Grande Valley (LRGV) one of the fastest-growing regions in the United States.

The border between the United States and Mexico is a gray area. Texas was part of New Spain and then Mexico for one hundred fifty years. When Texas won its independence, the border was never officially agreed upon. The Nueces Strip, the area between the Nueces River and the Rio Grande River, was a neutral zone for several years until the United States established the current border by military force. Spanish-speaking Texans whose forefathers held Spanish land grants are still ranching in the Nueces Strip.

The official border may be the Rio Grande, but the Border Patrol checkpoints where American immigration officials search every car and truck for illegal immigrants are some fifty miles north. There is a similar station on the Mexican side where you have to show a visa if you want to go any farther into the interior. In between these checkpoints is a hundred-mile-wide neutral zone where Tex-Mex biculturalism is an unremarked-upon fact of life.

Thanks to NAFTA and imports of tender U.S. beef, Tex-Mex fajitas are gaining in popularity in Monterrey. So are frozen margaritas, baby back ribs, taco salads, and ranch dressing. Meanwhile Mexican taqueros working out of taco trucks are serving gorditas, quesadillas, tripitas, mollejas, and other once-exotic Mexican fare all over the United States. Mexico and the United States seem to be blending into each other. What was once considered Tex-Mex fusion food has now become mainstream American and Mexican fare. Where do you draw the lines?

Try to imagine watching the Super Bowl without tortilla chips and guacamole.

On a road trip a few years back, I stopped at the Applebee's on I-30 in Texarkana. I had never been to a Texas Applebee's and I was surprised that the appetizer menu included chips and salsa, guacamole, chile con queso, nachos, and something called a "Chicken Quesadilla Grande," which turned out to be a tortilla stuffed with grilled chipotle chicken, melted cheese, onion, tomato, bacon, and jalapeños. I always figured that Applebee's, based in Kansas, represented the tastes of Middle America. So when did nuevo Tex-Mex catch on in Kansas?

On a 2007 trip to Monterrey, Mexico, to give a talk on Tex-Mex food to an international culture forum, my twenty-something guide, Lydia, a Monterrey native and talented music student, confessed that Applebee's was one of her favorite res-

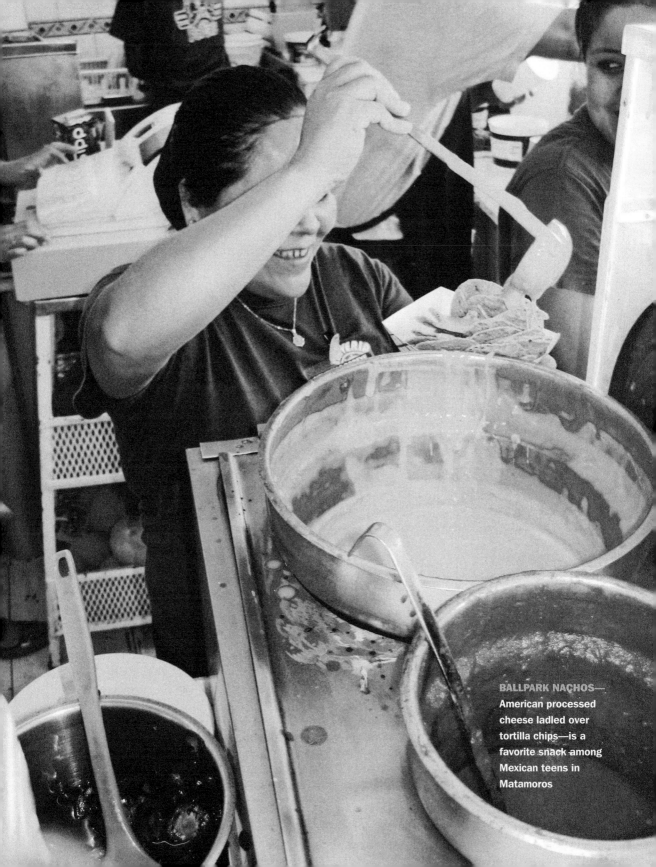

BALLPARK NACHOS—
American processed
cheese ladled over
tortilla chips—is a
favorite snack among
Mexican teens in
Matamoros

TO THE CHAGRIN of Mexican intellectuals, Taco Bell opened a location in Monterrey

taurants. Applebee's? In Mexico? Yes, it turns out there are more than forty Applebee's restaurants in Mexico, including three in Monterrey alone. And they are doing extremely well.

There was also a brand-new Taco Bell in Monterrey. When Taco Bell opened its first location in Mexico City in 1992, I felt compelled to go down there and eat a taco. I felt the same compulsion when I found out there was a Taco Bell in Monterrey in 2007. So I had Lydia give me a ride out there.

The restaurant was located in the Plaza Bella Mall near an H-E-B supermarket (a Texas grocery chain) in an affluent suburb on the city's outskirts. The bizarre menu featured such items as a "tambache" and a "tacostada." Thanks to the photos,

I was able to puzzle it out. A flour tortilla folded around a tostada and a ground beef filling is called a Crunchwrap Supreme at Taco Bell in the United States. "Tambache" is the made-up name Taco Bell has given it in Mexico.

And since rigid fried tortillas like the ones Taco Bell uses for its taco shells are called "tostadas" in Mexico, Taco Bell changed the name of their signature item from a "taco" to a "tacostada" to avoid getting into that whole what-is-a-taco debate with the Mexicans. Which would suggest that they ought to rename the chain Tacostada Bell in Mexico. While they are at it, they need to come up with a Spanish word for "spork," that combination spoon and fork they make you eat with. Combine *cuchara* and *tene-*

dor and you end up with the cutesy "cuchador." I like the macho "tenechara" better.

I sampled a few bites of a tacostada, a tambache, and a burrito with carne asado to see if there was any difference in flavor. But my fuzzy memories of Taco Bell cuisine are based on visits to the drive-through lane at three in the morning after the bar closed. As best as I can recall, this stuff tastes just as bland and gloppy as the Taco Bell junk I ate in the middle of the night back home.

Of course, the real question is: Why would people in Monterrey, Mexico, a city with awesome taque-rias, carnicerias, and street vendors, eat at Taco Bell? Looking around the restaurant, I would have to say that the answer has something to do with kids.

Three of the six tables taken were occupied by familes. I went over and sat down with Alfredo, Raquel, and their son Ronaldo, who were polishing off a burrito, some nachos, and a tacostada.

Papa Alfredo liked the nachos, which you can't get anywhere else around there. Raquel said that the picadillo is high-quality ground beef. "The food tastes good and it isn't as greasy as the tacos you get at a taqueria on the street," she told me. But Raquel confessed that the real reason they eat at Taco Bell is because young Ronaldo, a very picky eater, likes it.

"A lot of Mexicans are angry about Taco Bell coming here," Lydia told me on the drive back down-town. "They say it's watering down our culture." But Lydia shrugs it off. College students in Monterrey aren't quite as concerned about the encroachment of American fast food as the self-appointed guard-ians of Mexico's culinary patrimony are. Besides, like college students in the United States, she likes fast food. "We already have McDonald's, Carl's Jr., Burger King, KFC, Bennigan's, Applebee's, and Chili's, so it's not that big a deal," says Lydia.

Lydia prefers Carl's Jr.'s burgers to McDonald's, but she is most fond of Chili's, a chain that is already hugely successful in Monterrey. "I wouldn't go to Chili's on a date," she says, "But it's right there in the mall and it's so convenient." She always orders the boneless chicken-wing salad.

Fifteen years ago, after eating at the first Taco Bell in Mexico City, I wrote a story equating the arrival of Taco Bell in Mexico to the sacking of Rome. But that first Taco Bell quickly went out of business. And somehow the tradition of the taco, a food that traces its origins back to the dawn of time, remained pretty much unchanged.

I don't think the Taco Bell in Monterrey will have much luck selling ice to the Eskimos, either. Kentucky-based Yum Brands, Inc., which now owns the chain, is trying to expand internationally because Taco Bell sales are flat in the United States. If I had to guess why, I'd say Taco Bell is having trou-ble competing with the immigrant-run taco trucks and taquerias that are popping up all over the U.S.A.

Let the Mexican intellectuals go ahead and mock the talking Chihuahua. I say, may the best taco (or tacostada) win.

THE LATINO cartoon character Condorito on a wall paint-ing advertising a Houston *carniceria*

GUACAMOLE AT
Los Norteños in
Matamoros

All-American Guacamole

MAKES ABOUT 2½ CUPS

AMERICANS CHURN SOME FIFTY MILLION POUNDS OF AVOCA-dos into guacamole Super Bowl Sunday every year. But that is second only to the United States' number-one Mexican holiday—Cinco de Mayo.

- 4 ripe avocados
- 2 tomatoes, minced
- ½ teaspoon salt
- 1 clove garlic, minced
- 1 jalapeño pepper, seeded and minced (or to taste)
- 1 tablespoon freshly squeezed lemon juice
- ¼ onion, minced

Scoop out the avocado flesh and combine with the other ingredients. Mash by hand, in a molcajete, or in a food processor. Serve with tortilla chips as a dip or on lettuce as a salad.

Grilled Tomato Guacamole

MAKES ABOUT 2½ CUPS

A LITTLE GRILL CHAR ON THE TOMATOES AND GREEN ONIONS adds a lot of character to the guacamole.

- 2 tomatoes, hard stem area removed
- 4 green onions
- 4 ripe avocados
- 1 cup minced red onion
- 1 bunch of cilantro, stems removed and leaves chopped
- 4 teaspoons freshly squeezed lemon juice
- Salt

Put the tomatoes and green onions on a hot grill, turning often. Cook until the green onions have some color and the tomatoes are nicely charred, but not falling apart. Allow to cool, then chop the tomatoes and green onions.

Scoop out the avocados and combine the flesh with the green onions, tomatoes, red onion, and cilantro in a mixing bowl. Season with lemon juice and salt to taste. Mix the guacamole until everything is just incorporated, but still chunky. Serve with tortilla chips as a dip or on lettuce as a salad.

Chile con Queso

MAKES ABOUT 2 CUPS

VARIATIONS
ROTEL CHILE CON QUESO

Melt 1 pound chopped Velveeta chunks in a slow cooker or double boiler and stir in 1 can Rotel tomatoes with green chiles.

PACE CHILE CON QUESO

Melt 1 pound chopped Velveeta chunks in a slow cooker or double boiler and stir in one 16-ounce jar Pace Picante Sauce.

YOU CAN MAKE THIS IN THE MICROWAVE OR IN A DOUBLE boiler on the stovetop, but be forewarned the cheese quickly gets cold and unappetizing. That's why many people prefer to make chile con queso in a slow cooker. You ladle small amounts into the serving bowl as needed while the rest stays warm.

1 cup Velveeta cheese, cut into pieces
1 cup grated sharp cheddar
2 cups Picante Sauce (page 218)

Combine the ingredients in a microwave, double boiler, or slow cooker and heat until the cheese melts. Serve warm with tortilla chips or Frito brand corn chips for dipping.

VIVA VELVEETA

Invented in 1918 by Emil Frey, an immigrant from Switzerland, Velveeta was first marketed by the Monroe Cheese Company in Monroe, New York. Kraft Foods purchased the brand in 1927. It's not real cheese, but Velveeta doesn't deserve its reputation as an unhealthy food. Velveeta has never contained any trans fats. It is high in saturated fat and sodium, but so is cheddar cheese. In fact, Velveeta was originally advertised for its nutritional benefits because it's made with cheese, skim milk, and whey, a by-product of the cheese-making process that is considered to be a health food. It's still made with the same ingredients today. Real cheese doesn't melt and stay melted like Velveeta does—which is why most Texans consider it essential to chile con queso.

Tex-Mex Ranch Dressing

MAKES ABOUT 3 CUPS

HOMEMADE RANCH DRESSING IS VASTLY SUPERIOR TO—AND A
whole lot cheaper than—the stuff they sell in bottles at the grocery store. I
make this stuff in a plastic quart container and keep it in the refrigerator. My
kids slather it all over everything.

½ cup sour cream
½ cup mayonnaise
1 cup best-quality buttermilk
½ cup minced red onion
½ teaspoon minced garlic
¼ teaspoon dried thyme leaves
¼ teaspoon ground Mexican oregano
¼ jalapeño pepper, minced
2 green onions, thinly sliced
Salt to taste

In a medium bowl, whisk together all of the ingredients until well combined.
Cover and chill. The dressing will keep for about a week.

NOTE: Seed the jalapeño if you want to cut the heat.

SELENA, THE QUEEN OF TEX-MEX

Selena Quintanilla-Pérez grew up in Lake Jackson outside of Houston. She began her singing career in her family's Tex-Mex restaurant, Pappa Gallo. Selena spoke very little Spanish and had to learn the language to perform the music. She made Tejano music (as Tex-Mex music is known in northern Mexico), more popular than ever before. In 1994, shortly before her death, Selena gave a concert in Monterrey, Mexico, that electrified the audience and cemented her reputation as one of the most popular celebrities on either side of the border. There is a museum dedicated to Selena in Corpus Christi.

Carrot Pepper Salad

MAKES ABOUT 6 CUPS

THIS BRIGHTLY COLORED GARLICKY SLAW TASTES GREAT WITH grilled chicken and pork.

    4 cups grated carrots
    2 cups finely chopped red bell pepper
    ½ cup Tex-Mex Ranch Dressing (page 199)
    3 cloves garlic, minced
    Salt and pepper
    Fresh cilantro sprigs

Put the grated carrots and the chopped bell pepper in a mixing bowl. In a small bowl combine the ranch dressing and garlic and mix well. Toss the vegetables with the dressing. Add salt and pepper to taste. Allow to marinate in the refrigerator for an hour or more. Toss well and garnish with cilantro sprigs.

Chipotle-Curry Sour Cream

MAKES A LITTLE OVER 1 CUP

THIS IS A ZIPPY TOPPING FOR BLAND STUFF—AND AN AWEsome dip for raw vegetables, potato chips, and tortilla chips. Try it on grilled vegetables such as Char-Grilled Squash (page 209).

    1 cup sour cream
    1 chipotle chile, minced
    ½ teaspoon celery salt
    ¼ teaspoon ground white pepper
    1 tablespoon dehydrated onions
    ½ teaspoon curry powder

In a medium mixing bowl, combine all ingredients and mix well. Refrigerate for an hour to allow the flavor to develop. Serve cold with raw vegetables or chips.

Cilantro Cream

MAKES ABOUT 1 CUP

HERE'S THE COOL-DOWN TOPPING FOR SPICY DISHES. THIS stuff is ridiculously simple to make and impossible to stop eating.

  1 cup sour cream
  Juice of 1 lime
  ¼ cup chopped fresh cilantro leaves
  2 tablespoons chopped green onion

In a mixing bowl, combine the sour cream, lime juice, cilantro, and green onion. Refrigerate until ready to serve.

COCA-COLA IS the preferred beverage at the street-food stalls of Plaza Allende in Matamoros

Refried Beans

MAKES 3 CUPS

VARIATION
FRIJOLES NEGROS

Substitute cooked black beans.

COOK PINTO BEANS OVERNIGHT IN A SLOW COOKER OR, IF YOU don't have time to cook a pot of beans, start with a can of cooked whole pinto beans. If you do the refrying steps yourself, you'll still get a great homemade flavor.

¼ cup lard, bacon grease, or vegetable oil
3 cups drained cooked pinto beans
½ teaspoon salt
½ cup reserved bean broth
⅛ teaspoon freshly ground black pepper

Melt the lard in a large skillet over medium-high heat. Allow to heat for another minute, then add the beans and mash them for 2 minutes with a fork or potato masher. Stir in the ½ teaspoon of salt (or to taste). Add the bean broth and the pepper and continue mashing until the beans reach the desired consistency. Tex-Mex beans are generally chunky rather than soupy.

COOKING BEANS in a Dutch oven at the vaquero cook-off

Fajita Chili Beans

MAKES ABOUT 6 CUPS

THESE HEARTY BEANS ARE INCREDIBLY SIMPLE TO MAKE IN a slow cooker. While they make an awesome side with hamburgers or tacos, they can also serve as an appetizer. Have them cooked and ready to go and you can feed them to your guests while they watch you grill. Just don't be surprised if everybody keeps going back for seconds; chili beans are addictive. You will be amazed how fast this huge pot disappears.

1 pound pinto beans
2 cloves garlic, minced
½ pound cooked fajitas (or cooked ground meat)
½ cup chili powder
2 teaspoons granulated garlic
1 teaspoon granulated onion
1 tablespoon ground cumin
1 teaspoon ground Mexican oregano
2 teaspoons salt
Cayenne pepper or bottled hot sauce (optional)
2 tablespoons flour or masa harina

Rinse and sort the beans and place in a large slow cooker. Add water to 3 inches above the beans and add the garlic. Cook on the low setting overnight. Stir the beans and add water to maintain a soupy consistency while they cook. The beans are done when they are very soft but still maintain their shape.

Chop the cooked fajita meat into very small pieces and add to the cooked beans. Stir in the chili powder, granulated garlic, granulated onion, cumin, oregano, and salt. Add cayenne pepper or bottled hot sauce to taste, if desired. Cook for 30 minutes on the high setting, stirring now and then.

Dissolve the flour or masa harina in a bowl with a ¼ cup warm water. Pour through a strainer to remove lumps and add to the beans, stirring well to mix. Allow the beans to thicken for another 10 minutes before serving.

SHORTCUT: Substitute a commercial Texas chili mix such as Wick Fowler's or Carroll Shelby's for the seasonings. Use the amount specified for 2 pounds of chili meat.

VARIATION
CHILI BEAN FRITO PIE APPETIZER

Dump a small bag of Fritos corn chips into a bowl and pour a ladleful of beans over them, then top with shredded cheese and chopped raw onion. (If you want to be authentic, ladle the chili beans directly into the bag, then add the toppings.)

ROASTED CORN, or *elote*, grilled in the husk at the *tianguis* in Monterrey

Grilled Corn on the Cob
MAKES 6

YOU CAN PUT CORN ON THE COB DIRECTLY ON THE GRILL WITH-
out any precooking, but it takes forty-five minutes or so to get done. Here's a
recipe that's much faster but still gets great flavor from the grill.

    6 ears of sweet corn
    Cooking spray
    3 tablespoons Chile Butter (page 22)
    Sea salt and freshly ground black pepper

Put the unshucked corn in the microwave on high for 6 minutes or until the
corn is tender. Allow the corn to cool for 4 minutes. Peel back the husks and
remove all the silk. You can leave the husks on if you like the rustic look. Once
the corn is cooked to this point, you can hold it in the refrigerator for several
days and finish it on the grill when you like.

   To grill it, pull the husks back in a "ponytail," spray the corn with cooking
spray, and put the cobs on a hot grill. Cook, turning often, for 5 or 6 minutes or
until you get some nice char. Put the corn on a serving platter and spread all over
with Chile Butter. Season with salt and pepper to taste and serve immediately.

VARIATION
CORN OFF THE COB (ELOTE CON CREMA)
Remove the cooked
corn from the cob with
a sharp knife and mix
the kernels with crema
(Mexican sour cream),
mayonnaise, chili
powder, and parmesan
cheese. Serve in a bowl
as a side dish or an ap-
petizer.

Chile Grilled Pineapple

MAKES 4 SLICES

THIS IS A TERRIFIC COMPLEMENT TO GRILLED PORK, LAMB, and sausages.

4 teaspoons powdered red chile (see page 233)
4 slices fresh pineapple
Cooking spray

Sprinkle powdered chile on both sides of each slice of pineapple. Spray with cooking spray. Grill over medium heat until lightly browned, about 3 minutes per side.

Waldo Tailgaters Grilled Asparagus

SERVES 4 TO 6

THIS IS AN EXCELLENT QUICK-COOKING SIDE DISH. IF YOU have giant-size asparagus rather than the thin stalks called for in the recipe, the Waldo tailgating crew suggests you wrap each stalk in bacon.

1 pound trimmed thin asparagus
2 tablespoons olive oil
1 tablespoon minced garlic
¼ teaspoon ground Mexican oregano
Salt
Freshly squeezed lime juice
Chipotle-Curry Sour Cream (page 200)

Prepare the grill or comal. In a medium bowl, toss the asparagus with the olive oil, garlic, and oregano, and season with salt. Grill over medium heat, turning occasionally, for 5 minutes or until the asparagus are cooked through but slightly crunchy. Place the asparagus on a serving platter and sprinkle with lime juice and salt to taste. Serve with Chipotle-Curry Sour Cream.

Char-Grilled Squash

Makes 4 servings

GRILLING ZUCCHINI AND SUMMER SQUASH CARAMELIZES some of the sugars and gives them a great smoky, charred flavor. This works well with Cilantro Cream (page 201).

    2 zucchini squash
    2 yellow squash
    2 tablespoons olive oil
    Kosher salt to taste
    Freshly ground black pepper to taste

Wash and dry the squash. Cut the stem end off and slice the squash lengthwise in ½-inch-thick slices. Lay the squash slices out on a plate and sprinkle with oil, salt, and pepper. Place the slices on a very hot grill and cook on both sides until well done.

AT THE *AUSTIN* Chronicle
Hot Sauce Festival in Austin, the crowd lines up to
sample the hot sauces

CHAPTER 10

HOT SALSAS AND PICKLED PEPPERS

WE CALLED IT "HOT SAUCE" WHEN I WAS A STUDENT at the University of Texas in the 1970s. Unless you were speaking Spanish, then you said "salsa picante." At the grocery store, you looked for "picante sauce." Every Tex-Mex restaurant put a bowl of the stuff on the table. Most of them served it with tortilla chips. In the 1950s and 1960s, before tortilla chips were common, Tex-Mex restaurant patrons ate their hot sauce with buttered saltines. At a few old time-capsule Tex-Mex joints like El Patio in Austin, they still do.

When the Southwestern cuisine came along in the mid-1980s, food lovers started calling it "salsa" and chefs started taking it seriously. Exotic salsas from Mexico's interior made with all kinds of different chiles began to appear. Habanero salsas, green chile salsas, and salsas with exotic ingredients started turning up. I was the restaurant critic of the *Austin Chronicle* at the time, and I became a salsa connoisseur.

In 1990, the Travis County Farmer's Market sponsored a gardening competition. While the county agent was perfectly willing to judge peaches and watermelons, he wasn't willing to munch on jalapeño peppers. So Hill Rylander, who ran the farmer's market, called me and asked me to be the chile judge. I actually bit into some raw jalapeños and picked a winner. But I observed that since few people actually ate raw peppers, it might make more sense to hold a pepper sauce competition. Rylander loved the idea and resolved to hold it the next year.

Around that time, I wrote an article in *Chile Pepper* magazine calling Austin the hot sauce capital of the world. Predictably, salsa freaks in other cities disagreed. The *San Antonio Current,* a weekly newspaper in the Alamo City, chal-

lenged the *Austin Chronicle* to a contest—San Antonio versus Austin hot sauces—judged blind by top chefs. The first Hot Sauce Contest, as the event was originally known, was held at the Travis County Farmer's Market in 1991.

It was held outdoors on a Sunday afternoon in late August—the peak of the chile pepper growing season and the hottest part of the summer. We had a few musicians come and play and we asked a caterer to supply some beer. Austin won and a tradition was born.

There have been lots of changes in the intervening years; the San Antonio versus Austin format was scrapped and the contest was opened to people from anywhere in the world. We invited top Texas chefs like Stephan Pyles and Bruce Auden to be judges. And every year it got bigger. What started out as a contest with a few spectators turned into one of the best parties of the year. When ten thousand people showed up at the Travis County Farmer's Market one year, traffic came to a halt in north central Austin and we were asked to relocate.

In its seventh year, the *Austin Chronicle* Hot Sauce Festival, as the event is now officially known,

JARRO CAFE'S taco truck in Houston offers six varieties of salsa to choose from

AUSTIN CHRONICLE Hot Sauce Festival–goers sample the salsas

moved to a clearing in the woods of Waterloo Park. There was a lot of apprehension about the move, but as it turned out, the sylvan grove fit the event like an old pair of slippers. The stage tucked neatly between a pair of giant live oaks that kept the bands in the shade. An orderly procession of tents and booths kept the beer and hot sauce flowing nonstop. And plumes of sweet-smelling smoke rising from barbecue rigs, fajita grills, and green-chile roasters put a lovely blue haze on the edges. The contest has been held at Waterloo Park ever since.

The quality of the hot sauces entered has stayed consistent, though the variety has changed. We started out with red and green salsa categories. After a couple of years, we had to add a catch-all category called "special variety" to accommodate the Caribbean tropical fruit sauces that became popular in the mid-1990s. These weren't the sort of tortilla-chip dips that

we were used to. They were sweet and hot salsas that tasted best with grilled fish or grilled pork.

In recent years, we have received around four hundred salsas on average. I would estimate that around 70 percent of the entries are old-fashioned Tex-Mex picante sauces made with tomatoes. These can be divided into the fresh-tasting type frequently seasoned with cilantro, and a smoky-flavored type with smoked tomatoes and chipotles (and occasionally with liquid smoke). Green sauces made with tomatillos represent maybe 10 percent of the total. The other 20 percent or so are entered in the creative "special variety" category.

A curry-flavored Indian sauce won the special-variety category one year. Indonesian sambals, Thai peanut satay sauces, and fruity chutneys have all shown up in the special-variety category along with such oddities as dried cherry salsas, fig sal-

CLOCKWISE FROM TOP LEFT: hot sauce entries; frequent winner Jill Lewis, Austin Slow Burn; frequent winner Brian Rush, Tears of Joy; preliminary judges John Burnett (right) and Bud Kennedy (left)

sas, and one that contained coffee grounds. I still remember a dark orange–colored pumpkin habanero salsa from a little South Austin restaurant that won the "Special Variety–Restaurant" category in one of the first years of the contest.

That pumpkin salsa was so good, I went to the restaurant and asked for it some weeks later. Sadly, it turned out they only made it for special occasions. I still remember that salsa and that little restaurant. It was called Seis Salsas.

There was a circular salsa bar in the middle of the restaurant where you selected your condiments. And every day they put out six different varieties of salsa. I don't remember much about the food, but I remember the salsas. There was red and green, of course, and fresh chopped pico de gallo. There was a ridiculously hot brick-red chile de árbol sauce and there was always some variety of dark brown dried-chile salsa. And there was a wild card—it could be anything.

Seis Salsas disappeared in the mid-1990s. But the salsa bar concept is still around. It's an idea worth borrowing for your backyard barbecue. Line up five or six bowls and fill them with several salsas and other appropriate condiments. You'll be surprised how popular the add-ons really are. Salsa is the difference between good and great. And there's something about the audience participation involved in seasoning your own tacos that makes them taste better. Here are a couple of standard salsa recipes and a couple of wild ones to get you started. Feel free to experiment.

The Nineteenth Annual *Austin Chronicle* Hot Sauce Festival in 2009 attracted more than fifteen thousand festival goers. We judged around 425 hot sauces. When you perfect your own salsa recipe, come and enter your hot sauce in the competition.

Grilled Tomato Hot Sauce

MAKES 2 TO 3 CUPS

WHILE YOU'RE GRILLING, STICK SOME TOMATOES AND CHILE peppers on the grill and get some nice char flavor for your salsa. Grilling tomatoes over charcoal gives them an even better flavor than drying them in the oven. This is an outstanding everyday table sauce.

3 large tomatoes, quartered
½ onion, sliced in rings
2 cloves garlic, peeled
2 jalapeño peppers, halved lengthwise
1 tablespoon freshly squeezed lemon juice
½ cup chopped fresh cilantro leaves
Salt

Place the tomatoes, onion rings, garlic, and jalapeños on a hot comal and let them cook for at least 10 minutes, turning several times. Remove some of the charred skin from the tomatoes and jalapeños, then transfer the tomatoes, onions, garlic, and jalapeños to a food processor. Add the lemon juice and pulse for 30 seconds so the mixture remains chunky. Transfer to a bowl and add the cilantro. Season with salt to taste. Use immediately or refrigerate for up to a week.

Taco Truck Salsa

MAKES 2 TO 3 CUPS

I ONCE ASKED A TAQUERO RUNNING A TACO TRUCK FOR HIS salsa recipe. He looked at me like I was a dimwit. "You throw some tomatoes, a chile, an onion, and a clove of garlic in the blender with a little lime juice and turn it on," he said. So I tried it. And guess what? It tastes great. Sort of makes you feel silly for buying a jar of picante sauce at the store.

2 ripe medium tomatoes, approximately 12 ounces, coarsely chopped
1 jalapeño pepper, stemmed and coarsely chopped
½ large sweet onion, coarsely chopped
1 clove garlic
½ teaspoon salt
Juice of 2 limes

Place all ingredients in a blender or food processor, cover, and pulse until the mixture reaches the desired consistency, adding a little water if needed to make a puree. For milder salsa, remove the seeds and white membrane from the chile. Adjust salt and lime juice to taste. Use as a table sauce, taco sauce, or chip dip.

Picante Sauce

MAKES 2 CUPS

IF YOU WANT SOMETHING THAT TASTES EXACTLY LIKE THE bottled stuff at the grocery store, try this recipe for a homemade version of bottled hot sauce.

    10.75-ounce can tomato puree
    ⅓ cup chopped onion
    ¼ cup chopped fresh jalapeño peppers with seeds
    2 tablespoons white vinegar
    ¼ teaspoon salt
    ¼ teaspoon dried minced onion
    ¼ teaspoon dried minced garlic

Combine all ingredients with 1⅓ cups water in a pan over medium heat. Bring to a boil, then reduce the heat and simmer for 30 minutes or until thick. When cool, place in a covered container and refrigerate overnight. Use as a table sauce, taco sauce, or chip dip or as ranchero sauce in dishes such as huevos rancheros.

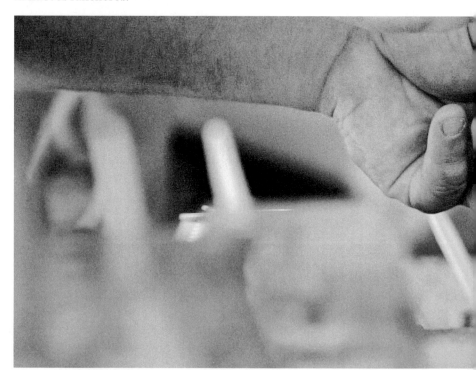

AUSTIN CHRONICLE **Hot Sauce Festival entries**

Salsa Verde

MAKES 2 CUPS

THE TART TOMATILLOS MAKE THIS A VERY GOOD SAUCE WITH fish. It's also a popular enchilada sauce with chicken.

1 pound tomatillos, husked and washed
1 cup chopped fresh cilantro leaves
3 fresh serrano chiles, seeded and minced
1 cup minced sweet onion
2 teaspoons minced garlic
Pinch of sugar
¼ cup freshly squeezed lime juice
Sea salt

Put the cleaned tomatillos in a saucepan and cover with water. Bring to a boil, then turn off the heat and allow the tomatillos to soak for 5 minutes. Remove from the heat, drain, and puree the tomatillos in a food processor. Add the cilantro, serranos, onion, garlic, sugar, and lime juice to the food processor and pulse three or four times to combine. Season with salt to taste.

CHILE PEQUÍN hot pepper sauce in a syrup dispenser

Homegrown Pico de Gallo

MAKES 2½ CUPS

THIS CHUNKY FRESH SALSA IS THE PERFECT WAY TO SHOW OFF your homegrown tomatoes in the summer. Use your favorite supersweet onions and the very best sea salt.

3 tablespoons freshly squeezed lime juice
½ cup chopped Texas 1015, Vidalia, Maui, or other sweet onion
2 cups chopped very ripe homegrown or heirloom tomatoes
2 tablespoons minced jalapeño, serrano, or chile pequín peppers
½ teaspoon sea salt
½ teaspoon freshly ground black pepper
2 tablespoons chopped fresh cilantro leaves
Dash of olive oil

Pour the lime juice in a medium bowl with the onion and allow to marinate for 20 minutes or more. Stir in the tomatoes and the remaining ingredients. Adjust the seasonings to taste. Refrigerate for at least 30 minutes. Serve cold.

Shaker Bottle Pequín Sauce

THIS IS THE OLDEST KIND OF PEPPER SAUCE IN TEXAS. IF YOU don't have a pequín bush in your backyard or in a nearby vacant lot, you can buy wild-harvested chile pequíns in a gourmet store or a Mexican market.

½ cup chile pequíns, washed and dried
½ cup white vinegar
Pinch of salt

Clean a previously used pepper shaker bottle with boiling water. (Or use a clean glass pancake syrup dispenser.) Pack the bottle with chiles. Heat the vinegar in a small saucepan over low heat until it steams slightly. Pour the vinegar over the chiles to the top of the jar and add salt. Allow the mixture to sit for a day before using. You can use the vinegar as a pepper sauce, or open the bottle to take out a few chiles. The bottle can be refilled with vinegar and salt about three times. Keeps refrigerated for 6 months or more.

Texas Red Grapefruit Salsa

MAKES 2 CUPS

TRY THIS TANGY SALSA ON GRILLED CHICKEN OR FISH. IT'S easy once you learn how to supreme a grapefruit.

2 Texas red grapefruits
1 medium tomato, chopped fine
1 cup diced green, red, and yellow bell pepper in any combination
1 jalapeño pepper, seeded and minced
3 tablespoons chopped red onion
1 tablespoon chopped fresh cilantro leaves
Salt to taste

Supreme the grapefruit (see page 149) and dice the sections. Combine with the other ingredients in a medium bowl and mix well. Allow to mellow for 30 minutes in the refrigerator for the flavors to combine.

TEXAS RED grapefruits

Kumquat and Pineapple Pico de Gallo

MAKES 3½ CUPS

THERE ARE A LOT OF SATSUMA, GRAPEFRUIT, AND MEYER LEMon trees in South Texas backyards, and believe it or not, there are also plenty of kumquat and loquat trees. One of my friends dumps paper bags full of kumquats at my house because I am the only person she knows who wants them. The sweet, sour little citrus makes an intriguing salsa that I love to serve with grilled shrimp.

1½ cups diced tomato
½ cup diced red onion
½ cup seeded and small-diced kumquat (unpeeled)
½ cup diced pineapple
½ cup chopped fresh cilantro leaves
¼ cup freshly squeezed orange juice
1 tablespoon habanero hot sauce
Salt to taste

In a medium bowl, combine all ingredients and toss. Cover and chill.

Ancho-Raisin Salsa

MAKES 2½ CUPS

THIS RICH, MOLE-LIKE STEAK SAUCE WAS INSPIRED BY A REC-
ipe that Robert Del Grande created for the California Raisin Marketing Board.
Try some of this stuff on a well-charred rib-eye steak!

2 cups leftover brewed coffee
1 ancho chile, stemmed and seeded
½ cup raisins
1 teaspoon cocoa powder
4 tablespoons (½ stick) butter
1 cup chopped onion
1 clove garlic, minced
1 tablespoon sherry vinegar
1 tablespoon Worcestershire sauce
1 teaspoon sea salt
½ teaspoon freshly ground black pepper
1 teaspoon freshly ground coffee

Warm the leftover brewed coffee in a saucepan over low heat. Tear up the
ancho and toast it lightly in a dry skillet. Mix the ancho and raisins into the
hot coffee and bring to a simmer. Turn off the heat and allow the dried chile
and raisins to soak until very soft, about 20 minutes. Stir in the cocoa powder.
Puree the mixture in a blender.

Melt the butter in a sauté pan over low heat and add the onions. Cook, stirring regularly, until they are soft, about 5 minutes. Add the garlic and cook for
another minute. Turn up the heat to medium and when the onions sizzle, add
the puree. Cook for 1 minute, then reduce the heat to a simmer. Stir in the vinegar, Worcestershire sauce, salt, and pepper. Stir in the ground coffee at the
last minute. Serve warm with grilled beef.

Pickled Jalapeños

MAKES ABOUT 1½ POUNDS (DRAINED)

THE ICONIC, INDISPENSABLE CONDIMENT FOR EVERY TEX-MEX
meal is a bowl of pickled jalapeños. Here's how to make them at home.

- 2 tablespoons olive oil
- 1 small onion, sliced thick
- 5 cloves garlic, peeled and quartered
- 15 jalapeño peppers, approximately 1 pound, rinsed
- 1 pound carrots, peeled, rinsed, and sliced ½ inch thick (approximately 2 cups)
- 1¼ cups cider vinegar
- 1 tablespoon pickling salt, plus more as needed
- 1 teaspoon ground Mexican oregano
- 4 bay leaves
- White vinegar as needed

Heat the oil in a large soup pot over medium-high heat. Add the onion and
sauté for 3 minutes, then add the garlic. Continue cooking for another minute
or two until the onions are soft. Add 8 cups of water and bring to a boil. Add the
jalapeños and carrots and cook for 5 minutes, or until slightly softened.

Add the cider vinegar, 1 tablespoon of pickling salt, Mexican oregano, and
bay leaves and simmer for another minute. Remove from the heat and allow to
cool. Remove the jalapeños, carrots, and onions with a slotted spoon or tongs
and place in a glass jar (you may need several). When the cooking liquid has
cooled, cover the vegetables with liquid until the jars are three-quarters full.
Add a tablespoon of pickling salt to each jar and fill to the top with white vinegar. Cap the jars and keep in the refrigerator. Will keep for several months.

RESTAURANT SIGN in a
remote area of the Mexican
desert across the Rio Grande
from Big Bend National Park

CHAPTER 11

CHILE GLOSSARY AND MAIL ORDER SOURCES
Chile Peppers

I N A DEPARTURE FROM THE STANDARD SPELLINGS USED IN Merriam-Webster, this book uses *chile* or *chile pepper* to refer to the pods, and *chili* or *chili con carne* to refer to the dish. • Unfortunately, the names used for specific chiles vary across the United States. The big green poblano chile, and its dried form, the ancho, are essential to the Tex-Mex cooking style. *Poblano* and *ancho* are well-known names in Central Mexico, Texas, and most of the United States, and are also the names used in such standard reference materials as Mark Miller's Great Chile Poster and in nearly all Mexican cookbooks.

But the poblano is confusingly called a *pasilla* or *ancho* in both the fresh and dried form on the Pacific Coast of Mexico. Since most of the Mexican Americans in Southern California come from Oaxaca and the Pacific states, their nomenclature is used in Los Angeles.

Grocers on the Eastern Seaboard, however, buy their chiles from the L.A. Produce Terminal. So, in an odd migration of misunderstanding, food stores in New York, Boston, and Washington, D.C. often use the Oaxacan nomenclature for chile peppers.

Fresh Chiles

F RESH CHILE PEPPERS ARE USU-ally harvested in the green stage. Fully ripened red chiles are most often used for drying, but they also turn up fresh in the supermarket for a brief period in the fall. The following fresh chile peppers, listed from mildest to hottest, appear in this book.

ANAHEIM

ALSO KNOWN AS THE LONG GREEN Chile by New Mexicans and West Texans (until it turns red and becomes the Long Red Chile), the Anaheim has a pleasant vegetable flavor and ranges from slightly warm to medium-hot. Anaheims are generally roasted and peeled before they are used. The name comes from a chile cannery opened in Anaheim, California, in 1900 by a farmer named Emilio Ortega, who brought the pepper seeds to California from New Mexico.

In New Mexico, the Long Green Chile is further subdivided by region of origin. The two most common names encountered are Hatch and Chimayó. Hatch chiles are grown in the southern part of New Mexico (around the town of Hatch) from certified seed sources and are graded according to heat. Mild green Hatch chiles are often roasted and peeled, then eaten like a vegetable.

Chimayó chiles are the older, more traditional

DRIED CHILES and corn
shucks for tamales at
the Monterrey *tianguis*

chiles grown in the northern part of the state (around the town of Chimayó) from seeds that have been saved from the previous harvest. Chimayó chiles are treasured for their superior flavor and unpredictable heat, but they are becoming increasingly rare.

POBLANO (ALSO CALLED ANCHO OR PASILLA)

FATTER AND WIDER THAN THE ANAheim, the poblano is a darker green and has a richer flavor. It is one of the most commonly used chiles in Central Mexican cooking, both in its fresh and dried forms (see "Ancho"). Poblanos are named after the Mexican city of Puebla, where they probably originated. They are generally slightly hot and are usually roasted and peeled before use.

JALAPEÑO

HOT, GREEN, AND BULLET-SHAPED, the jalapeño is the classic Tex-Mex hot pepper and one of the world's best-known chiles. Originally grown in Mexico, it is named for Jalapa, a town in the state of Veracruz. The fresh jalapeño has a strong, vegetal flavor to go with the heat. We prefer to cook with fresh jalapeños, but the jalapeño is most widely consumed in its pickled form. Besides hot sauce, a bowl of pickled jalapeños is the most popular condiment on the Tex-Mex table. For a recipe, see page 227.

SERRANO

SIMILAR TO THE JALAPEÑO, the serrano is hotter and smaller. Most Mexicans claim that serranos have a fuller, more herbaceous flavor. Since the vast majority of jalapeños are pickled, the serrano is actually the most widely used fresh chile pepper in Mexico and Texas.

PEQUÍN

ALSO KNOWN AS *PIQUÍN, CHILIPIQUÍN,* or *chiltepín,* this tiny chile grows wild throughout southern Texas and northern Mexico. Although *pequin* seems to be a corruption of the Spanish *pequeño,* meaning "small," the Spanish name itself is probably a corruption of *chiltecpin,* a Nahuatl word meaning "flea chile," a reference to both

its size and sting. Because its seeds were spread by birds rather than by cultivation, pequíns are considered the oldest chiles in North America. In northern Mexico, they are collected in the wild and sold in markets, where they fetch more than almost any other kind of chile. They are sometimes dried and preserved for year-round use. A pequín bush can be found in almost any backyard or vacant lot in southern Texas, and pequíns are very common in Tex-Mex home cooking. Because they are not grown commercially, they are seldom found in restaurant cooking or in grocery stores. If you find some, you can substitute three or four fresh pequíns for one serrano or half a jalapeño.

HABANERO

THE WORLD'S HOTTEST PEPPER, the habanero should be treated with respect. It has a wonderful apricot-like flavor and aroma, but it must be used in small quantities and handled with care. The habanero was introduced to Mexico from the Caribbean and is named after Havana, Cuba (*habanero* means "someone from Havana").

RAJAS

ROASTED PEPPERS THAT HAVE BEEN seeded, peeled, and cut into strips are called *rajas.* They're used as an ingredient in some recipes and as a condiment for fajitas.

Dried Chiles

THE FOLLOWING DRIED CHILE PEPPERS, listed from mildest to hottest, are used in this book.

ANAHEIM, NEW MEXICAN CHILE
(FOUND IN POWDERED FORM ONLY)

ANCHO (ALSO CALLED PASILLA)

THE DRIED FORM OF THE POBLANO chile, the ancho is very dark brown and wide (in fact, the word *ancho* means "wide" in Spanish). Anchos are the fleshiest of the dried chiles, and their pulp combines a mildly bitter flavor with a sweetness reminiscent of raisins. They are usually mild, although occasionally one will surprise you with its heat. Mulattos are closely related and are a suitable substitute.

CHILE DE ÁRBOL

LITERALLY "TREE CHILE," THE chile de árbol is a small, red, shiny chile about three inches long with a thin tapering body. It has a high heat level and is often chopped and simmered with tomatoes to make a hot table sauce.

GUAJILLO

TAPERED WITH A SMOOTH, SHINY, reddish skin, the guajillo has a tart, medium-hot flavor. When soaked and pureed, it gives foods an orange color. Dried Anaheims are also sometimes called guajillos, but they are much milder.

PASILLA

LONG AND SKINNY WITH A BLACK, slightly wrinkled skin, the pasilla has a strong, satisfying flavor and can range from medium-hot to hot. The name comes from the Spanish *pasa,* meaning "raisin," a reference to the appearance of the skin. On the West Coast of Mexico, and hence in Los Angeles, they also call fresh green poblanos "pasillas."

CHIPOTLE

THIS IS THE SMOKE-DRIED JALAPEÑO. Small, wrinkled, and light brown, chipotles have an incredibly rich, smoky flavor and are usually very hot. Smoking jalapeños to preserve them has been common in Mexico since long before the Spanish arrived. The original Nahuatl spelling, *chilpotle,* is also sometimes seen.

We prefer to use dry chipotles, but you can also buy them canned, and canned chipotles are acceptable in most recipes. Obviously, you can't make chile powder from canned chipotles, but you can use them for purees. Canned chipotles are already soaked in some kind of sauce, usually a vinegary adobo. Just stem and seed them and puree them with some of the sauce from the can.

CAUTION: HANDLING CHILE PEPPERS

It's wise to wear rubber gloves when handling jalapeños, serranos, and, especially, habaneros. Get a little juice from the cut-up pepper on your face or in your eyes, and you can count on ten minutes of sheer agony. If you don't have rubber gloves, use a piece of plastic wrap to hold the pepper while you cut it. Clean the knife and the cutting board immediately with hot soapy water. If you get pepper juice on your hands, try soaking them for a few minutes in a mild bleach solution.

Roasted Peppers (Poblanos and Green Chiles)

TO PREPARE PEPPERS: LIGHTLY OIL THE surface of the peppers. Roast peppers over a flame or under a broiler until charred on all sides. Set aside in a plastic bag for ten minutes to allow the steam to loosen the skin from the pepper. Peel off the charred skin and discard. Slit one side of the pepper down the middle, remove and discard the seeds, and set the peppers aside until serving time. Peeled, roasted peppers can be stored in the refrigerator for two or three days or for up to three months in a resealable plastic bag in the freezer.

Powdered Chiles

YOU WON'T BELIEVE WHAT A DIFFERence it makes to use your own fresh powdered chile instead of commercial chile powder. You can blend a combination of dried chiles for a more rounded flavor. Or you can grind various chiles and keep them separate. Start with five dried chiles such as anchos, guajillos, or pasillas. Prepare the chiles by removing the stem and seeds. Toast the peppers in a dry skillet over medium heat for five minutes, turning frequently, until dry and crisp but not burned. Process the pepper in a coffee grinder until it becomes a fine powder. Store in sealed spice bottles or baby-food jars.

Mail-Order Sources

ALL OF THE INGREDIENTS IN THIS BOOK ARE COMMON THROUGHOUT THE Southwest and most of the rest of the country. If you have a Mexican market in your town, you should have no trouble finding everything you need. If you can't find some of the fresh produce we use, the item you're looking for might just be out of season. If you live in an area where Mexican ingredients are unavailable, try these mail-order sources.

ADAMS EXTRACT AND SPICE

www.adamsextract.com

Pinto bean seasoning, ancho chile powder, chipotle powder, whole dried chile pequíns, New Mexican chile powder, New Mexican green chile flakes, granulated jalapeño, cracked black pepper, and mesquite-smoked black pepper.

BOLNER'S FIESTA SPICES

www.fiestaspices.com

Fajita seasoning, brisket rub, pork rub, chicken rub, rib rub, and wild game rub; dried chiles and powdered chiles.

TEXJOY

texjoy.com

Steak seasoning in regular, spicy, and Worcestershire flavors.

TEXAS SPICE COMPANY

texas-spice.net

Powdered chiles and seasoning blends; private-label spice blends.

GOODE COMPANY

www.goodecompany.com

5015 Kirby, Houston, Texas 77098

800-627-3502

Spice mixes and seasonings, charcoal starter chimneys, and all kinds of barbecue tools and Texas gifts are available here. Call for a catalog.

WWW.TEXMEX.NET

Lots of Tex-Mex products and free manufacturers' recipes are available here, as are anchos, spice mixes, and a full line of Rotel products.

PENDERY'S

www.penderys.com

1221 Manufacturing Street, Dallas, Texas 75207

800-533-1870—Catalog $2

Molcajetes, chiles, ground cumin, chili powders, and Mexican oregano are all in the catalog.

SUPERBLY SOUTHWESTERN

www.hotchile.com

3816 Edith NE, Albuquerque, New Mexico 87107

800-467-4HOT, 505-766-9598

A source for whole or chopped frozen roasted green chiles, New Mexican chile powders, and dried chiles.

BELLVILLE MEAT MARKET

www.bellvillemeatmarket.com

Grill rubs, spice blends, and some of the best sausage in the state.

THE SPICE HOUSE

www.thespicehouse.com

1512 N. Wells Street, Chicago, Illinois 60610

312-274-0378; fax 312-274-0143

Chiles, chili powders, barbecue seasonings, and other exotic spices are available from this outstanding spice merchant.

MO HOTTA MO BETTA

www.mohotta.com

The "world headquarters of hot sauce" has thousands of varieties of hot sauces, pepper sauces, barbecue sauces, salsas, wing sauces, jerk sauces, and more. Note that real Jamaican jerk sauce isn't a liquid that pours from a bottle. It's a thick herb paste that comes in a jar you can get a spoon inside of. Walkerswood and Vernon's Jamaican jerk sauce are recommended.

Credits

Index